"Anyone can be a triathlete. It's one thing to s   make others believe it. Hilary Topper proves by sharing her own journey from the sofa to the start line and beyond. If you think you're too out of shape, too unathletic, too old, too heavy, or too anything to become a triathlete, this inspiring book will change your mind."
–Matt Fitzgerald, author of *Life Is a Marathon*

....

"Hilary manages to convert a personal story into a must-read insight on the power of embracing a journey in performance. Her inviting and accessible narrative highlights her bravery, but also the fabric of what a performance journey entails. Through challenge, fear, and adversity, Hilary emerges to amplify her health, performance, and life, becoming an inspiration to many. If you are one of those people who believe you could never or shouldn't, then read this book and get going on your own journey of excellence."
–Matt Dixon, IRONMAN Master Coach, CEO and founder of Purple Patch Fitness, former professional triathlete, and author of *Fast-Track Triathlete: Balancing a Big Life with Big Performance in Long Course Triathlon and The Well-Built Triathlete*

....

"Hilary Topper discovered the empowerment of endurance exercise through triathlon training. Her writing celebrates the achievements of those who were not born with the talent to win races. In her new book, Hilary relates the many training and racing experiences that enriched her life. She knows that the sport of triathlon will be there to help her process the next challenge that comes along."
–Jeff Galloway, running coach and creator of the Run Walk Run® method

....

"Hilary Topper's book is inspiring on so many different levels. For an experienced Ironman like myself, I found the races to be exciting. For someone who is still sitting on the couch, it encourages and motivates you to go beyond your comfort zone and do something that is extraordinary. This is a must-read for both current triathletes and those looking to try something new."
–Peter Shankman, best-selling author and two-time IRONMAN athlete

"Whether you have been an athlete your entire life or sport is something new, this book will resonate with and inspire you. Though maybe for many of us victory is about winning medals and being first, this book captures the power of the most meaningful successes of all. The wins are not measured by your place at the finish line, but rather by those that allow you to conquer your own personal, limiting beliefs so you can be the best version of yourself. Hilary's powerful story will transform you and empower you to push yourself beyond the imaginable."
–Nina Sadauskas, three-time Olympian swimmer, CEO and founder of Delfina Athletics

....

"Hilary Topper has written a must-read for anyone willing to undertake the seemingly impossible task of completing their very first triathlon. Reading this book transported me immediately back to the blood, sweat, and tears I experienced as a first-time triathlete. Hilary delivers a delightful guide packed with rich emotional detail, unvarnished truth, and the practical step-by-step information to encourage any reader to push outside their comfort zone and reach for the stars."
–Julie Moss, IRONMAN Hall of Fame and SATriathlon Hall of Fame inductee, author of *Crawl of Fame*, race announcer, and keynote speaker

HILARY JM TOPPER

From Couch Potato to
ENDURANCE ATHLETE

A Portrait of
a Non-Athletic
Triathlete

Meyer & Meyer Sport

British Library of Cataloguing in Publication Data
A catalogue record for this book is available from the British Library

From Couch Potato to Endurance Athlete
Maidenhead: Meyer & Meyer Sport (UK) Ltd., 2022
ISBN: 978-1-78255-240-6

Aachen, Auckland, Beirut, Cairo, Cape Town, Dubai, Hägendorf, Hong Kong, Indianapolis, Maidenhead, Manila, New Delhi, Singapore, Sydney, Tehran, Vienna

Member of the World Sport Publishers' Association (WSPA), www.w-s-p-a.org

Printed by Versa Press, East Peoria, IL
Printed in the United States of America
ISBN: 978-1-78255-240-6
Email: info@m-m-sports.com
www.thesportspublisher.com

The stories in this book reflect the author's recollection of events. Some names, locations, and identifying characteristics have been changed to protect the privacy of individuals. Dialogue has been recreated from memory.

CONTENTS

FOREWORD

Becoming a triathlete was an easy transition for me. I was a distance swimmer in college. My senior year, I qualified for nationals, earning All-American distinction in the one-mile race. At the end of the season, I wasn't ready to hang up my athletic career. My college swim coach suggested I try a triathlon, so I did. I knew nothing about triathlon training but learned the basics, got a bike, and signed up for a sprint triathlon in western Maryland, close to my school. I won the triathlon overall and was hooked. Now I had something else to compete in!

I spent the next few years racing in Maryland and Delaware and eventually on Long Island when I moved back home. My first Ironman was in 2001, at the age of twenty-four. I won my age group and qualified for the Ironman World Championship in Kailua-Kona, Hawaii!

Success came easy for me in the sport, where I eventually finished second in my age group and as the fourth amateur overall in Kona before the age of thirty. That's when I decided to race as a professional. I raced for the Zoot Triathlon Team for another four years before hanging it up. During that time, I had some successes, placing as high as sixth in Ironman Austria and fourth in Ironman Lake Placid. I always coached athletes on the side, but in 2014, I decided to start my business, Iron Fit Endurance, taking it to the next level.

My reasons for triathlon racing were simple: compete to win and qualify for Kona. As I started coaching, I became aware of the many other reasons people fall in love with the sport. Instead of competing for a podium spot, many athletes do it to challenge themselves. Many do it hoping to make cutoffs, hoping to get to that finish line at the end of the race.

Coaching opened me up to a whole new world. I've been inspired by so many athletes who've had to overcome so much just to get to the race, let alone complete it. I'm in awe of so many of these athletes, and I've found myself in tears as I've witnessed them coming off the bike with minutes to spare before the cutoff time or finishing the race minutes before the official time cutoff would've declared them a DNF ("did not finish"). These are the athletes who make up so much of triathlon racing today, and with each person, there's an inspiring story behind it.

Hilary Topper is one of those athletes who chose the sport of triathlon for different reasons than I did. Hilary never considered herself an athlete, far from it! She never competed in sports as a kid and barely went to gym class. At the age of 48, she decided she would try running, and she fell in love with it. When I met her, in 2015, she was just getting into triathlon. She had recently learned to swim and had just bought her first tri bike. She didn't feel confident in her abilities; she worried about being last in the events she signed up for, yet she was determined to do them anyway.

When I put myself in her shoes, I'm truly inspired. As I mentioned, the sport was an easy transition for me, one I found success in right away. It fit into my life; I was an athlete before I got into the sport. For Hilary, it was a complete reinvention of herself. Looking at Hilary's past, you can see that she's always challenged herself in diverse ways, defying odds, pushing past her insecurities and other people's viewpoints that she "can't" and she "won't." Instead, she shows that she *can* and she *does*. She became a successful business owner despite others telling her she wouldn't succeed, and then she transformed herself from a non-athlete to a *triathlete*.

Imagine immersing yourself in something that's so out of your comfort zone and opposite to anything you've ever done before. Something you and others doubted you could ever accomplish. How scary would that be for you? Could you do that at this point of your life? Reading this book will motivate you to do just that!

I've had the pleasure of coaching Hilary for the past six years, and she's an inspiration, always finding the next insurmountable goal to push herself toward and always forging ahead and remaining positive no matter the obstacle in her way (and Hilary has had plenty of obstacles).

PREFACE

There are so many running and triathlon books on the market today. But none address a huge group of individuals of which I am proud to be a part of, the "back-of-the-packers."

While we were not graced with superb natural ability like some athletes, we train just as hard, if not harder, than the elite or age-group athlete. Yet, every race we participate in is a challenge because of time. How so? Well, the question is never about whether we can do the endurance activity, because we can. The question is whether we can finish the race within the set time constraints.

Just think about how long we're out on the course doing what we do. Some of us will reach the finish line of a Half Ironman in exactly eight hours and thirty minutes or a full Ironman in seventeen hours, while most elite or age-groupers do these distances in half that time.

Sometimes I feel like there's a bit of shaming going on when it comes to the back-of-the-packers. We do these activities, and it takes us a long time to accomplish them, but we don't get much respect. Most of the spectators have gone home by the time we finish events, and yet, we've finished them, just like our counterparts.

In "Back-of-the-Pack Runners Have More Fun," a *Medium* article, Michael Horner writes, "After the race, I was talking with a friend who was much faster than me. As I spoke of the mud while trying to peel my socks off my feet, he said the trail was in good condition and still frozen when he went through." That's what it's like to be a back-of-the-packer.

He continues: "In the back of the pack, everybody is relaxed and concentrating on living and enjoying the race. The only stress is whether we will make it through each of the time cutoffs."

At *300 Pounds and Running*, a blogger concurs: "I started running in 2012 and races were not friendly to bigger, slower runners like me. And it hasn't gotten any better since. As a back-of-the-packer runner, I still feel neglected and disrespected."

There is a stigma to being a back-of-the-packer. But what other athletes don't realize is that we're doing this for our health and well-being. We're doing this to get off the couch and be out in the community. We're doing this for fun because we love it. And it doesn't matter if we come in last because we still accomplished our goal.

This book is an adaptation of my triathlon blog. I have been maintaining a running journal of all my races and experiences during the past ten years. Although this book will appeal to any new runner or experienced triathlete, I dedicate it to those of us out there who are in the back of the pack—the non-athletes who try so hard it hurts. The ones who want to place but may never do so. This book is for you.

I hope my journey motivates you.

Thanks for reading!

ACKNOWLEDGMENTS

I want to thank so many people for their help with this book. For starters, I want to thank my children, Zoey, Derek, and Dan. You have been my rock, and I love you guys. I want to thank Brian for not giving me a hard time about doing what he calls, "crazy things" and always being there for me. I want to thank Mindy for her love and support through the years. Thank you to Ed, Andrea, and my nephews for cheering me on during those Florida races.

Special thanks to Madeline Silverman, who is one of my dearest friends. I asked her to read the book before publication and she had some amazing suggestions. Thank you to Lisa Gordon who is my partner at HJMT Public Relations, my friend, and confidant.

Thank you to Thomas McLean with Cardinal Publishing Group and Liz Evans at Meyer & Meyer Sport. I appreciate you both for believing in me and my story.

I also want to thank all the coaches who have helped me along the way. Special thanks to my running group, triathlon team, and all the Long Island runners and triathletes that are always ready for the next challenge! I love you guys!

And thank you for being you!

"Your wings already exist all you have to do is fly."
–Staci Kushin Blanket, Ironman, New York

CHAPTER 1

My Entrée Into Sports

I wasn't always a triathlete. As a matter of fact, I didn't do anything athletic until about 10 years ago, when I realized I was getting older and fatter.

The beach and ocean were in our backyard, as I grew up in Long Beach, New York. When I was young, I went to the beach with my parents, but I was never allowed in the water past my knees. "The ocean will swallow you up," my mother would tell me. So, I was always afraid. Even when I went with my high school friends to the beach, I would never go in past my hips. I was just too scared of the rip current.

When I was a kid, my dad taught me to ride a bike. My earliest memory was of him running alongside the bike and then letting it go. My mother was always a nervous person. She didn't like any of us doing any type of physical activity, including cycling. She was afraid we'd get hurt.

I can still hear her saying, "Don't go out too fast or too hard."

When I was eight, my mom took a job at Camp Wildwood. She worked at the canteen; my sister, Lori—although underage—worked as a waitress; and my brother, Ed, went to camp there. I attended Camp Mikan-Recro, a set of sister–brother camps with my friend, Philip.

Philip's mother and my mother were best friends, and his mother helped get my mother a job at Camp Wildwood.

At the wee hours of the morning, "Reveille" would play, and the girls from Mikan and the boys from Recro would jump out of bed, put on our bathing suits, and head over to the freezing lake, where we were forced to jump in. That was one of my earliest recollections of being in the water, and it wasn't a pleasant experience. They tried to teach us how to swim, but I wouldn't put my face in the water. So, I didn't learn.

Growing up in Long Beach, the second and third graders would get bused to the recreation center once a week to learn to swim. Again, I didn't want any part of learning to swim. I wanted to splash around with my friends. And that's how that went.

In 1980, when I was in high school, I cut gym as much as possible. I thought gym was a big waste of time and hung out in the smoking lounge with the rest of my friends. Anyone could smoke back then, and smoking lounges were popular in many high schools.

If I participated in PE, I was picked last, and that always made me feel horrible. I don't know why it did. I mean, I couldn't catch a ball, so why would I be picked first?

One day, when I was still in high school, a group of friends and I went for a bike ride. We planned to cross over the Atlantic Beach Bridge, a small bridge a few miles from my home. My mother didn't want me to go. "But all my friends are going," I told her. She finally gave in but was not happy.

As we were riding past the West End of Long Beach through Atlantic Beach, my friend, who is now my husband, Brian, passed me, and I hit his back wheel. Both of our bikes flipped, and I was knocked unconscious. I was taken to Long Beach Memorial Hospital and told I had a concussion. When my mom got there, she said, "I told you so!"

My bike riding days were over for a while.

****

My parents were terrible cooks. Every night for dinner, we were served burnt steak, dried-out chicken, or noodles, cheese, and butter. One time, my dad caught a fish from the bay at the end of my block. He took it, put it in one of my mother's "good" pots, and boiled it up for dinner. I couldn't and wouldn't eat it. I ran up to my room and put the covers over my head.

Back then, I weighed ninety-eight pounds and ate bologna and ketchup every day with a grape Hi-C followed by a Devil Dog. Processed foods were the in thing, and no one spoke about how unhealthy they were for your body.

That's the way I lived my life—barely eating, or eating junk, with little to no exercise.

****

My childhood wasn't a happy one. At the time, no one really talked about child abuse, yet my parents practiced it on me both mentally and physically every day.

My parents married young and had all three of us young, and I don't think they were ready. My mother ruled the house, and she was very controlling. She was overweight, insecure, and I believe, looking back, probably bipolar. She always thought other people were better than we were. We were never good enough. I was never good enough.

My mother had a lot of love, but she showed it only sometimes. Later in life, she openly showed it to her grandchildren, but she didn't show it to me during my childhood. There were days when she was amazing and I loved to talk with her, and then there were other days when she screamed at me for no reason, telling me I was an "idiot" or "stupid." I never knew which person was going to come out that day.

My mother would put me in front of the mirror and tell me I was ugly. When I was recently talking with my brother about this, he recalled that she'd compare me to a troll, saying that the troll was prettier than me.

Although I never really saw my dad when I was growing up, because he worked three jobs, my mother knew how to get my dad going. If any of us did something she didn't like, she'd rattle my dad and tell him to get the belt. That belt was used often, and it affected all of us in different ways.

My dad was totally devoted to my mother. She was his life.

I don't know why, but for some reason, he found it very difficult to share his affection with us kids. I wanted it so bad. And yet, there were times when he would come up to my room as I was going to bed, and he would tell me he was going to take me on all these exotic trips. I believed him. I wanted him to take me away from the horror I was living, and I prayed that one day he would. Unfortunately, the trips never happened.

Growing up, I also never had any privacy. My mother didn't believe in doors or locks. For the longest time, the five of us lived in a one-bedroom apartment on the first floor of our home. Eventually, the upstairs tenants moved out, and we took over the entire house.

When we moved upstairs, my bedroom doors were immediately taken off. The only one who had any privacy was my sister. She lived in the front room with two doors. My mother insisted that she needed her space because she was older. Lori was the black sheep in the family. Yet, she got all the attention from my mother. I resented Lori for it.

One time, I got into a fight with my mother. I ran upstairs to my bedroom with no doors and remember talking on the phone with my boyfriend, telling him what happened. My dad came upstairs and took the phone out of my ear and started beating me with the phone. My boyfriend was still on the line!

****

I never had any encouragement at home or in school. I remember my Long Beach High School English teacher telling me I would never amount to anything. And my parents didn't want me to go to college.

They wanted me to get a job as a secretary and retire at 55. Exercise was also never a part of that picture.

My entire childhood, I was led to believe that I wasn't smart enough, pretty enough, or worthy enough. I was told that the bad things that happened to me didn't really happen. They were a figment of my imagination. My mom would always say that the disturbing things I experienced weren't real; they were just a "bad dream."

I still attempted to find out what I was good at, even though I never received the encouragement to do so. I tried lots of things while I was growing up, like playing the flute in the marching band or taking art classes. Nothing stuck. I felt like I did a lot of things but wasn't good at anything. I was depressed and had frequent thoughts of suicide. I felt utterly alone, unwanted, and a complete failure. No one seemed to care to tell me differently.

****

I journaled consistently throughout my life. That was my secret place where I could share whatever I wanted without being judged. I loved to write and share my experiences in my notebook.

So, when blogging surfaced back in the early 2000s, I jumped in full force. I've been blogging ever since. Recently, my husband made a joke to my son that "Mom writes about everything she experiences." Haha—it's true!

****

When I left my parents' house, my biggest motivation was that I didn't want to live my life like them. I didn't want to struggle for money. I didn't want to feel like I was nobody. I wanted to be somebody.

Since my parents didn't encourage me to go to college and I wanted to go, I spent most of my time working. I worked full time to pay for college and went to school at night. My life was mostly hard work and very little play. But when I did play, boy did I play hard!

I drank, smoked, and did everything in between. I wanted to escape the reality in which I was living. But when it was time for work, I was on time and focused.

After I graduated from college, I worked for several years at some of the top PR firms in the country and then decided to go back to school on the weekends for my master's degree, while continuing to work grueling seventy-to-eighty-hour workweeks. I still didn't feel good enough, even after I got my master's degree. The voices of everyone from my childhood would sneak in and tell me I was worthless, no matter how much I achieved. No matter how hard I worked, it never felt good enough.

I remember, when I was a young girl, that my paternal grandfather told me to "reach for the stars." I couldn't understand how I could do that coming from a home of negativity, but as I got older, I understood what he was saying. I needed to constantly dig deep and get that encouragement from within, because I knew I wouldn't get it anywhere else.

In the 90s, I raised my daughter and my son while starting my own business. I worked all the time while raising my children, and I felt fulfilled. And, when I didn't work, I devoted every second to them. When I had to, I even brought my kids with me to business meetings. Every day, there was a networking breakfast, a lunch catch-up, and a dinner meeting. I loved to outsmart my competition, and I enjoyed networking and meeting new people. I was happy for the first time in my life.

HJMT, my business, grew and grew. There were a few downturns— once after 9/11 and another after the stock market crash of 2008. But every time my firm got knocked down, I picked it back up. After every curveball that came my way, I made sure we came back stronger.

About ten years ago, something changed. I was fully absorbed in my work, but it just wasn't making me happy any longer. I didn't want to battle those curveballs anymore. I was sick and tired of the ups and downs of the business. And I needed a change.

****

This is my story of how I transformed my life at forty-eight years old. It begins when I first started running and continues through my triathlon journey. I share the lessons I learned, the injuries I overcame, and the goals I achieved and failed to accomplish along the way. It's real and raw, filled with laughter and tears. My story is meant to remind you that no matter how often you're pushed down, you alone can be the resounding force to pick yourself back up and move forward. If I inspire one person, it'll make this journey worth it.

2009-10

"Just get out the door first and see what you can do today."
–Bernice Imei Hsu, Ironman and ultrarunner, Washington

CHAPTER 2

Learning to Run

In 2008, when the market crashed, I had to terminate many of my employees. It pained me to do so, but I had no other choice. In 2009, though, after I published my first business book, I saw a real uptick in business again. I was starting to feel good. We moved into a beautiful office in Melville, New York. I had my name on the sign at the business's entry, in the lobby, and I even had my own private parking spot. Although people said to me, "You finally made it," I didn't feel that way. Things were looking up, but the more they looked up, the more stressed out I was. My business success just wasn't giving me the high it used to. I was sick of the up and downs. And all this stress made me pack on weight. I needed something to release my nerves in a positive way and thought running could be the answer.

I was always intrigued by the runners along the Wantagh State Parkway (a road that ran north and south across Long Island). It looked so fun, graceful, and a great way to clear your head. I would drive my car and go out of my way just to watch the runners. There was something magical about watching people run. I wanted to try it and see if I could find that magic too.

JANUARY

For some reason, unknown to me, I thought my first step should be to join a gym. I had never been a gym member before, and I thought I could change my life by hiring a personal trainer.

After joining a gym, I sat with Tom, my new personal trainer, for nearly an hour, talking about nutrition and exercise. Now I was pumped and ready to work out. We scheduled an appointment.

The following day, I was at the gym at 8 a.m., ready to go. I warmed up on the treadmill. I didn't really know what I was doing. I had to have someone help me turn it on, and I started to walk.

After some time, Tom came down to get me. We went upstairs to the weight room. He showed me the equipment, and I worked out for an hour.

Everything seemed so hard, but I was determined to work it through. In the back of my head, I also reminded myself that I had to lose fifteen pounds!

When the session was over, I went home and crashed. I was out for about two hours in a deep sleep. When I woke up, I told myself that I could do this and kept going back for more.

FIRST SPIN CLASS

Morris, a professional peer, and I drove together to an Entrepreneurs' Organization (EO) conference in Atlantic City, New Jersey. We were both members of EO and part of the same forum. On the ride there, he talked about spinning and how he really enjoyed it. "And you know you burn 600 calories in an hour," he said.

Six hundred calories . . . hmm . . . sounds good, I thought. I need to burn a lot of calories to lose this weight! So, when I found out that the gym had spin classes, I signed up.

A few weeks later, when I attended the class, some of the other participants were extremely nice and tried to calm my nerves. "You know, if the class is going too fast, you can change your resistance," one woman told me. "You'll love it," said another.

As soon as the instructor walked in, I mentioned that I was new to this. He helped me adjust the bike and get set up. "Just start cycling," he told me and walked to the front of the class, turned on the music, and started the program.

Okay, I thought to myself. This is it . . .

Here I was, sitting on a bike in Oceanside, New York, spinning away. As we climbed hills, the instructor told us to increase the resistance. We were on a steep hill for a long time. It felt like hours but was only minutes. "OK, now stand," the instructor said, and the whole class got up on their bikes and rode standing up. "You can do it!" he screamed out. "Come on, even you rookie over there," he said pointing to me. "Now come back down to first or second position and keep up the pace. I want you to count. You should be between 16–20 reps."

He walked over to me. "How many reps?" he asked.

"I'm sorry," I said all out of breath with sweat dripping down my face, "I don't know what you're talking about." He was very patient and explained what he meant.

After the class, I thanked him and went to my car feeling exhausted yet energized. I immediately thought of calling Morris.

"Hey, did I wake you?" I asked. "No," he said. "What's up?" "I took a spin class and have a quick question—what's first position?"

TWO MONTHS LATER . . .

Since joining the gym, I didn't take a break. I exercised every day for at least a half hour to an hour and a half. Yes, my clothes were fitting me better. And yes, I had so much more energy. And yes, I even lost about eight pounds.

So why was I complaining? I was always in pain!

Whenever I trained, it was tough. Every time the trainer asked me to do something else, I felt as if my legs, then my stomach, then my arms would fall off! I'm not kidding. It hurt!

I wondered if it would ever get easier.

Every time I walked into the gym, I got my card scanned, and the woman or man behind the desk said, "Enjoy your workout!" Enjoy my workout? Who does? I could barely get motivated to go to the gym, let alone enjoy it. Every time I went, I would feel sore. Sometimes after a tough workout, I felt as if I couldn't even walk! And talk about the next day... I was in so much pain. Now, you may say, "No pain, no gain." And that's true, but I thought it would get easier. The more I was doing, the harder it was getting. I asked my trainer if he was in pain every day.

"Every day, something hurts me," he told me.

Sometimes I think that liposuction would have been the better alternative, and then I think this is the natural way to get it done. But have a good workout? Or enjoy your workout? Are we having fun yet? Or are we just suffering through it until it's over?

JULY

I had never run a day in my life. After almost seven months of training at the gym, I started to run on the treadmill. When I ran my first mile, I was so excited. One morning, my trainer told me to warm up on the treadmill. I went out very slowly, at a pace of around 4 mph, almost a walking pace, but I was able to run the whole mile. I was so impressed with myself. The next day, I did it again, even faster! A year before, I'd been unable to run a block, and now I was running a mile on the treadmill!

I decided to take my running to the next level and run outside. Boy was that hard! After a block or two, I slowed down and found it difficult to do a mile, much less a few blocks!

MEETING BECKY

I met Becky at a local women's group. We went to the same high school, but she was a few years older than me, so we never met. Becky was personable, friendly, and always had a smile on her face.

I told Becky about my interest in running. She wanted to know if we could run together. I was totally intimidated. I barely could run a mile, and Becky was already a marathon runner. Why would she want to run with me?

"Hilary, it's just one minute of running, one minute of walking until you no longer have to walk, and then you're a runner," she said.

Becky was an athlete. She was a college professor and coach. She played volleyball in high school and went on to play in different tournaments. Why would she want to run with me, Ms. Couch Potato?

But she wouldn't let it go. One day, after she called again, I said yes. I was so nervous. Would she judge me? Would I make a fool out of myself?

Our first run was difficult. We decided to walk and run the boardwalk in Long Beach. The boardwalk was 4.2 miles round trip. We ran a little, we walked a lot, and we slowly made it to the end of the boardwalk and back. It took almost two hours. I was totally exhausted, but I did it. For someone who'd never run a day in my life to run–walk four miles was a big accomplishment.

As Becky and I started to run once a week, we decided to set a goal and gear up for a half marathon. She convinced me that a good goal was a half marathon. Haha . . . I'd never even run a 5K, let alone a half, but we saw an ad in *Runner's World* that there was a half marathon at Disney World.

"What do you think?" I asked Becky via Facebook DM.

"I love the idea," she wrote. We both signed up.

Hey, it could be fun, right? I'd never raced before, but how hard could a Disney race be? Mickey Mouse and Donald Duck? Come on, it'll be a breeze, I thought.

AUGUST

Now that I was up to three miles on the treadmill at NY Sports Club, I decided it was time to run with my kids. I wasn't running errands.

And I wasn't driving them from activity to activity. I was on the middle school track running with them.

We collectively decided that we'd run three miles. My daughter, Zoey, who was on the high school track team, sprinted during the first mile. She was convinced that she wouldn't be able to make it. My son, Derek, on the other hand, thought it would be a breeze, but it wasn't. We all did it. We all ran twelve times around the track for a total of three miles. I ran and I walked. I certainly didn't do three miles without stopping!

The best part—I spent quality time with my kids.

SEPTEMBER

It was a cold and windy day. The sky was bleak. Becky and I were on a schedule. We needed to run six miles outside to keep up with the program we got from *Runner's World* magazine.

I walked out of my house to meet Becky halfway between our homes. When we met up, we started running. The two of us ran to and up the Long Beach Boardwalk and passed other runners and cyclists. We saw the empty beach and clear blue water, a series of apartment buildings, and then the end of the boardwalk!

"Should we keep running west?" I asked.

"No," she said. "Let's turn back, and then we'll run all the way to your house. That should be about six miles."

I trusted that Becky knew what she was talking about, since she'd already run a full marathon the previous year in New York City.

At about the fourth mile, she handed me liquid energy called "Gu." I sucked it down and swallowed it. It tasted like black cherry but had a thick consistency. Although it upset my stomach, I got a very quick boost of energy, which helped carry me all the way home.

I don't know if it was my new sneakers, the weather, or the "Gu," but the funny thing was, that day, I felt like I could have kept running forever.

Becky and I both trained hard for the Disney World Half Marathon. It took us quite a few months, but we finally thought we were ready.

Lesson Learned

If you want to make a change, start today. Don't let the voices in your head bring you down. If you put your mind to it, you can do it. Take a small goal and accomplish that first. Slowly build up each week until you reach your goal. Don't wait until tomorrow; start today.

CHAPTER 3

Running Firsts

After I had trained with Becky for a few months, we decided to sign up for a 5K AIDS and Cancer Run Walk in Oceanside, New York at Oceanside Park. As soon as Becky sent me the information, I sent my registration in with a donation. I felt ready to run a 5K.

When we got to the race site, it seemed a bit disorganized. We noticed tons of bagels in paper bags and coffee cups still in plastic. There was a lot of commotion. Becky and I decided to go with the flow and just hang out in the back while the volunteers set up.

We were excited to run this race in preparation for the Disney World Half Marathon.

After some time, we got our numbers. Becky got number #717. I got number #668. This was the first time I had gotten a race number, and I had no idea what to do with it! Becky explained that it attaches to your shirt via safety pins.

When the race was about to start, we were asked to go to the starting line. Someone rang a bell, and the runners were off. The first mile was torturous. My legs were aching, and my body was just run down. Becky and I stayed together.

Becky encouraged me the whole way. Every time I wanted to slow down or stop, she told me to keep going. "You can do it," she said. I dug deep and got through that first mile without stopping. I needed to prove to Becky and to myself that I could do this.

The second and third miles felt easier. My legs felt less pain, and I felt that I was in a rhythm. When my breathing got erratic and heavy, Becky told me to concentrate on slowing down my breathing. "Breathe in and count one, two, three and breathe out and count one, two, three . . . ," she said.

At each mile marker, we were told our time and given a cup of water. Volunteers cheered us on.

When we were a quarter mile away from the finish line, we could hear the announcer screaming out the runners' times. Becky and I decided to sprint to the end.

Hearing the cheers made me run faster. I got to the flag in thirty-seven minutes and was impressed with myself for being able to do it without stopping.

It was 10 a.m., and the volunteers started walking around serving sandwiches and wraps. I couldn't eat much but decided to have a banana to keep my energy level up.

We waited patiently as the announcer called the winners to come up and receive their trophies. After that, the race organizer went to the microphone and called out numbers to receive prizes. It seemed like everyone was winning something. Becky won a trip for two to Fire Island. The woman next to me won a case of energy drinks. I ran to the bathroom, and I could hear someone saying, "She's in the bathroom."

I came out and found out that I'd won a paper bag full of leftover, stale bagels that hadn't been eaten earlier in the morning. I covered up my number and ran to my car!

Although the 5K was fun, I wanted more of a challenge to keep pushing myself. So, I signed up for the 10K Turkey Trot in Long Beach.

NOVEMBER—MY FIRST 10K

When I woke up, I heard the weatherman on the radio say it was forty degrees Fahrenheit. "Wow, that's cold," I thought. Now, how should I dress for the Turkey Trot race?

I decided to layer up with a windbreaker. I knew I would be hot, but I wanted to stay warm until the last possible moment. I also had asthma, and I feared that the cold would make me wheeze.

Since Becky was ill, I decided to do the race alone. My husband, Brian, who had recently taken up running, asked if he could join me. Personally, I didn't think he'd be able to keep up, but I told him sure. He was injured the year before, having shattered his kneecap in seven pieces. He had to have two surgeries to repair it, and he was out of commission for a long time. I was impressed with the progress he'd made but was still skeptical. Most people in his situation would have just sat back and watched TV. He was determined to get better.

When we got to the start of the race, we sat in the car. It was freezing outside. "Let me go to the bathroom before the race starts," I said. I got in the long line for the ladies' room. I started to see people taking their places. Hmm, should I go or hold it in until after the race? I went. When I came out, Brian told me that the race had already started. "Oh no," I said, and we both took off.

We ran faster than normal trying to catch up to the pack, but we were unable to. We ended up running alone.

I'd been averaging a fourteen-minute mile but, during this race, I ran my first mile in eleven minutes. Although I set a fast pace, Brian kept up with me. I was pleasantly surprised.

The air was cold, and at first, it hurt my lungs to breathe. I also realized that I was breathing heavier than normal. I remembered what Becky told me about breathing. "Just breathe in and out to the count of three: one, two, three—breathe in, one, two, three, breathe out . . ."

After the second mile, my breathing adjusted, and I started to feel very light on my feet. I didn't feel the pain in my legs or my feet. I felt as if I could run forever. The race took us through the town and on the boardwalk.

After a lot of uneventful miles, I saw the finish line. I started to sprint. It felt incredible. Brian sprinted too. We crossed the finish line in one hour and seventeen minutes. I was so proud of him for coming such a long way, and he said he was proud of me for being a "road warrior."

I laughed. It's amazing what your body can do. I'm the person who cut gym and almost failed it, and here I was, in my late forties running a 10K. Pretty cool, huh?

WHEN I FIRST MET BRIAN

I met Brian in middle school. We both grew up in the same town and had the same friends. He was tall, thin, had thick, wavy brown hair, and wore glasses. He always dressed nicely and was well liked by everyone. I found him thoroughly attractive both inside and out, and when we both graduated college, we decided to get married. We'd been married almost twenty-five years at that point when, as a lark, he signed up for the NYC Half Marathon. He got in! I did not.

So, I got an entry, too, by donating to Team for Kids, a New York City charity teaching disadvantaged children all about running.

Now we really needed to train together! Brian and I ran the New York Road Runners Ted Corbitt 15K in Central Park. We thought the Corbitt race would be great preparation prior to the half.

The night before, my husband and I went out to dinner.

"Should we order a bottle of wine?" he asked me.

"Well, we're really not supposed to drink before a race," I said. "Isn't it going to dehydrate us?"

We both looked at each other and decided to order the wine. A week prior to this, we were talking with a couple from our hometown who were marathon runners. They were telling us a story about how they ran better after having a hangover. I was told, though, that when you're training, you shouldn't drink, but I didn't know why.

My husband and I shared a bottle of wine. After that, we went back to the hotel room—we stayed in Manhattan overnight—and went to sleep. I was up all night from the alcohol. Every two hours, I woke up.

At 5 a.m., the alarm went off. I had the worst headache, felt nauseous, and was in no mood to run 9.3 miles.

But my husband convinced me to run. "You have to practice for the half marathon in Disney," he said.

We drove uptown, parked the car in a lot, and walked over to the park. It was thirty degrees out, but the wind made it feel much colder. When we arrived at the starting line, the race was moments away from beginning. We could hear the national anthem, and as soon as the announcements started, we were in line ready to go. We both finished the race, but we got injured. Brian's back was hurting him for weeks after that, and my knee was a mess.

How would we ever run the NYC Half Marathon?

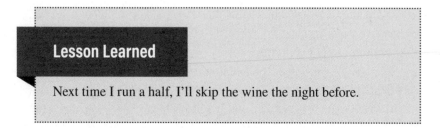

Lesson Learned

Next time I run a half, I'll skip the wine the night before.

2011

"You may not be the fastest, but you are faster than everyone sitting on the couch wishing they could run that race."
–Danielle Motz, half marathoner, New York

CHAPTER 4

Turning Point

JANUARY

Becky and I flew to Disney in early 2011 to run the Disney Half Marathon. We stayed at the Beach Club by EPCOT. When we checked in, we had to wait a long time in the lobby. Our flight had been delayed, so we ended up arriving a few hours after check-in time.

By then, our room was given to someone else, and it took a few hours for a new room to be cleaned. We felt jetlagged and exhausted from all the training. When we finally got the keys, it was after midnight.

As soon as I walked into the room, I felt nauseous. I threw up. I still wasn't feeling great from the Ted Corbitt, and the travel made me feel even worse. It was a disaster!

We realized we probably should have flown in a couple of nights before and gotten a good night's rest and recovery before going into this race. Here we were supposed to run our first half marathon together, but knew it wasn't going to happen that day. It felt like the odds weren't in our favor before it even began. So, after sleeping in, we ended up going shopping instead of running the half marathon. (By the way, there's a great outlet center in Orlando.)

RECOVERING

It took Brian and me a month or so to recover from the Ted Corbitt 15K. Still, we started to feel better and continued to train. We had a hefty goal and wanted to make sure it happened. I didn't care about time, I just didn't want to be pulled off the course because I was too slow. And I certainly didn't want to get injured again.

One of my high school friends who also became a runner later in life said to me, "You should try to beat your time every time you race, even if it's only a minute."

But to be honest, at that point, I really didn't care. I just wanted to finish.

FEBRUARY

During our training for the NYC Half, Brian, my teenage son, Derek, and I went to Seattle. We were going skiing on a vacation at Mount Rainier, and before that we stopped off to tour the city. Amazingly, I found a race called "Fun Run with Super Abe" at Seward Park in Seattle. So, I convinced my family to do it with me.

When we got to the park, we were absolutely freezing. While we sat there with the heat blasting, we noticed a few "Abe Lincolns" walking around. We looked at each other and laughed. The race was in honor and celebration of Abraham Lincoln's birthday, and there were quite a few people on stilts dressed as Abe Lincoln.

I really thought that Seattle was warmer than New York, but I was wrong. The wind chill made it feel as though it went through my entire body.

Everyone around us seemed to be standing in the sun warming up. Brian, Derek, and I walked over to the crowd and tried to stretch. I started to go up and down on my toes to stretch out my hips.

Suddenly, a woman with a bullhorn walked over to the crowd. "We will be starting in five minutes," she said. "Please make your way over to the start line now."

We all walked over to the starting line. Moments later, the race began.

It was a beautiful run. The sky was blue with no clouds. We ran around Lake Washington. It was amazing to be running with locals around a park that I had never been to before. Everyone was so friendly. I felt at home!

As I ran, I watched the houses across the lake turn into big buildings as the city of Seattle appeared in my range of vision. What a modern city! The buildings were interesting and held my attention until I saw one of the "Abe Lincolns" on the trail. He pointed up.

I looked up and saw a steep hill. Derek had already run up it. He was gone. I started to worry about him and hoped we would see him at the end.

Brian and I looked at each other and shook our heads as we started to run up the hill. It was so steep and looked physically impossible. I didn't know how Derek did it.

The hill went on a while until there was a big turn, and then everyone went downhill.

It took two miles before I warmed up. Those first two miles were always a "killer." The backs of my legs were burning, and my shins were throbbing and, since the air was so cold, my asthma kicked in, and I started to cough endlessly.

Despite this, the last mile was much easier. The sun started to heat up the park and I kept running until I had to walk again. I was just at the three-mile marker when I saw another "Abe Lincoln" pointing toward the finish line.

As I approached the last quarter mile, Mount Rainier came into view beyond the lake, providing an inspirational moment. The mountain seemed to jut out of the water in the shape of a volcanic cone, like pictures I have seen of Mount Fuji in Japan. It was so magnificent that it motivated me to finish the race.

Interestingly, after this race, I posted photos on my Facebook page. One of my running friends said, "No matter what or how you feel, when you run through the finisher's chute, make sure to put your hands up and pose." And that's how my signature pose first started. After that, I posed for every race, no matter how I felt.

****

When we came back home, Brian and I started training hard, gearing up for the 2011 NYC Half Marathon. We trained on the Long Beach Boardwalk and ran solely around Lido Beach and Long Beach, where our home was at the time. Looking back on this, we didn't even know how to train. We just ran as far as we could with lots of walk breaks in between.

Running started to become an addiction for me. I thought about the woman at the gym telling everyone to have a good workout. Now I started to understand what she meant.

Running with Brian was intense. He ran faster than me and complained that I went out too slow. He used to complain that I didn't push myself. I didn't. I didn't really think it was necessary. Maybe it was my mother in my head telling me to not go out too hard or too fast. Whatever the reason, I didn't push at that time.

On the weekends, I continued to train with Becky. I loved telling her stories about my life, and I enjoyed hearing her stories about her family and friends.

MARCH AND THE NYC HALF MARATHON

I was nervous about the NYC Half. It was my first big event. I kept thinking that I was a non-athlete trying something I wasn't equipped to do. What do I know about running? I come from a family of non-athletes. I felt like an imposter.

Brian and I stayed in the city the night before the race. This time, a bottle of wine was not on the menu!

We woke up early and were eager to go. We turned on the television to find that the temperature was in the thirties, and it was windy.

We quickly got dressed wearing layers of clothes. I ended up wearing my running pants and my plum jacket. Over that, I proudly wore my Team for Kids bright yellow tank top with my number on the outside. We threw on some old fleece sweaters for throwaways and hurried down Wall Street in search of the express train.

It was exciting to see all the runners on the subway. Most of us were packed in like sardines.

When we finally got to 103rd Street, a group of us walked off the train, up the stairs, and headed directly to Central Park. With every step, I got more and more excited that this day was finally here, and I was going to attempt to run my first half in three hours or less.

We were in the brown corral. My husband and I had similar numbers, and we stood together and waited for the opening ceremony. All the runners were talking with us. Everyone was friendly and looking forward to the race. I opened my Nike app and started to listen to the music on my iPod.

We took off our fleece sweaters and put them on the side of the corral. We had heard that volunteers picked up the items after the race started and donated them to the homeless.

When the bullhorn blew, we were off. I was determined to get through Central Park. The park was a 6.2-mile loop. I was told that if you didn't get through the park within a certain time frame, they would pull you off the course.

I didn't want to stop. So, I didn't. I kept running. Then suddenly, my iPod stopped working. There was no music. Could I possibly do this without music? Yes, I could!

The crowds, the environment, and the entertainment on the streets were my music. I was determined to concentrate on making this run happen. I repeated to myself, you can do this, you can do this, you can do this!

As I ran through the park, I looked up at the buildings and looked over at the reservoir. It was so amazing! I felt so small in this large place, and, at the same time, I felt like I was running in my own town.

I have always loved New York City. I lived there for a few years before moving back to Long Beach.

The music and entertainment at several spots along the route made the whole experience fun, especially when I passed a big chicken playing a stand-up bass.

The hills were tough. I found them very hard, and yet I didn't want to stop running for fear of being disqualified. I kept it up. I saw the children who were benefiting from Team for Kids, and they screamed my name, which motivated me to go on.

I was breathing so heavy, and another runner ran alongside me who said that there was only a little more to go before we exited the park and then, "It's all downhill from there." She was very encouraging and got me through the end of the park.

Coming out of the park and onto the streets of Manhattan was amazing. There were lots of people cheering.

I think the best part was when we ran across 42nd Street. There were so many people on the street, and a DJ was loudly playing Bruce Springsteen's "Born to Run." The music and the people energized me. The neon signs and the billboards felt as if they belonged to the runners. The only bad thing about this part of the run was that there were potholes everywhere, and I was afraid I was going to fall.

At mile nine, my legs were hurting, my feet were swollen with blisters, and my hips and knees were killing me.

Once I got to the West Side Highway, my motivation was low. We were close to the Hudson River and the wind was blowing hard against us. Suddenly, out of nowhere, a Team for Kids coach, Ryan, started to run alongside us.

"How are you doing?" he asked.

"I'm hurting, but determined to finish," I said.

"You will finish," he said. "You're doing great. Just two more miles to go."

At this point, my husband sped past me. He was running so fast I could not catch up, even if I wanted to.

During the last two miles, Ryan ran with me. He encouraged me to keep running and not to walk. He told me that I was working twice as hard as everyone else because my stride was short.

He tried to get my mind off running by asking me what I was going to eat after the race and what I did the night before the race. As we ran together, people were screaming, "Go Hilary, go Team for Kids!"

"You're almost there," he said as we approached the "800 meters to go" sign. "It's just a quarter mile, and you know that's nothing."

I sped up when I saw the 400 meters sign. I ran faster and crossed the finish line in exactly three hours.

As I caught my breath, members of the New York Road Runners club took my photo, and then provided me with a medal and a blanket.

We saw another Team for Kids coach who told us to come to the Team for Kids booth where we were given water and greeted as if we were old friends. The coaches were hugging me and giving me words of encouragement that I'd achieved what I'd set out to accomplish. This was a big achievement.

I looked over at the river and saw the Statue of Liberty. I started to cry. This was important to me, and I didn't think I could make it, but I did.

Lesson Learned

Most of the fear about races is in your head. Get out of your own way. Make sure to encourage yourself. You are amazing just for signing up. If you train, you are ready. Trust the training. There is no better feeling than crossing the finish line!

2012

"I think of all those who have passed on in my life. Sometimes I do a particular group, like those lost in the military, or work friends, or family, etc. I think of each person, then I dedicate the race to those who are no longer with us. I am racing for them . . ."
–Brad Kirley, 9x Ironman, finisher of fifty-two 70.3 triathlons, Virginia

CHAPTER 5

Shattered Life

The year started off uneventful. I continued to train and received an entry to the NYC Half Marathon in March. This time, I decided to do the half marathon on my own, and I loved the experience. About a mile from the finish line, I saw my kids. They were screaming my name, but I couldn't push. I felt like I was going to crash. That was when Derek ran beside me and coached me in. Running through the finishers chute with Derek was amazing. If he hadn't run alongside me, I would have given up, but he gave me the motivation to keep going. I felt proud of myself for finishing a touch race.

Since Lori and I celebrated our birthdays on April 25 and my mom celebrated hers on April 26, I wanted to spend my fiftieth with my mom. It doesn't matter how old you are or how your parents did or didn't treat you, you always want your parents' love and approval. I know I always felt that way. I wanted to hear that they were proud of me and proud of the woman I had become. I also knew my mother wasn't doing well physically, and I wanted to take this opportunity to be with her, hug her, and even try to resolve some of our past issues.

I left the rest of my family at home and flew to Ft. Lauderdale to spend the long weekend with my parents. I hadn't seen my parents for a couple months, and I wanted quality time with them. I couldn't think of the last time we had celebrated my birthday together. As this was a big one for me, it meant a lot to be with them.

APRIL

My mom and dad lived in Tamarac, Florida. They had moved there when my son was still a baby. Although I knew it was good for them, I was upset that they wouldn't see my kids grow. My mom had been sick for a while and wasn't doing that well. She was grossly overweight and had a severe food addiction. When she was a child, she had polio and was in an iron lung for more than a year. At fifty, the polio returned and between that, her autoimmune disease, her serious asthma condition, along with COPD, she had a lot of physical problems.

These days, the post-polio was getting the better of her, and she was finding it difficult to walk and to breathe. This left her glued to a wheelchair with an oxygen machine. She wasn't old. She was only seventy-four. Mentally, she still had so much life to live, but physically, she was going downhill.

A few moments after I arrived, my mom said, "Hil, can you videotape me and your father? I want to talk about my life and leave a legacy for my grandchildren." I pulled out my phone and started recording.

They both talked about their lives, and in the video, my mom said, "And you Hilary, well, I'm not worried about you. You will always land on your feet. It's everyone else, I'm worried about."

As I was recording, I heard my sister's voice. "Hey, Hil, I'm here!" I thought I was going to jump out of my seat. I couldn't believe Lori came down to Florida from Long Island, too!

Lori, who was exactly four years older than me to the day, was tall with curly brown hair. Her curls were so tight, like my father's mother's hair. She kept it curly. Lori had a golden-brown complexion and rarely had to wear makeup. She went up and down with her weight. At this point, she was heavier than she had been. Lori was a true sun worshipper. She would literally turn dark brown from the sun. She was beautiful.

She had a natural beauty that would turn heads. Throughout my entire life, I never saw Lori without a boyfriend. As for her social life, if she had one glass of wine, she became the life of the party.

My mother and others would compare us with each other. Some thought she was prettier, others thought I was prettier. I never understood why they did that, but they did. It made me feel uncomfortable when others compared us, especially my mother. She would say I had the brains and Lori had the beauty. She would tell me that I didn't need her support, but Lori did because Lori had a hard life with two bitter divorces. Although it made me angry to hear because I needed my mother's attention too, I shrugged it off and accepted it. My entire life, I only wanted my parents' love and acceptance—even at the sake of my own self-esteem.

When Lori and I were younger, we competed against each other, but as we got older and had our own children, we became very close. Lori was my best friend. We talked almost every day about life, love, and friendships.

Spending my fiftieth birthday with my mom and my sister was wonderful. It was one of the best birthdays I had in a long time. We did absolutely nothing. Just spent the time sitting in my mother's apartment laughing, going through old letters and memorabilia, and talking about the past. It was the last time I saw my mother alive.

JUNE

I thought my mother would make it through the summer and I booked a trip for my kids to see her one last time. Right before we were going out there, her hospice nurse called me and insisted I come a few days earlier. I called Lori. "I'm coming with you," she said.

And with that, Lori, her daughter, Jessica, and I got on a plane and headed down to Florida. If all was good, my kids would be on the plane that we had originally scheduled a couple of days later. At this point, my daughter was a junior in college, and my son was in high school.

As we were landing, I looked out the window and saw the most magnificent rainbow I had ever seen. I knew at that moment that my mother passed.

When the plane landed, we got a text message from our brother, Ed, who lived in Florida with his wife, Andrea, and their three sons, that she died. "You missed her," he wrote. I will never forget the drop in my heart and the feeling that my life was shattered. Lori and I were screaming and crying in the Fort Lauderdale airport. The people there must have thought we were nuts. Lori kept yelling, "Why didn't you wait? Why didn't you wait?"

****

I started to run more and more to work out the loss of my mother. I had so many unresolved issues that I never got to talk with her about and, as a result, it was all bottled up inside of me.

I continued to run with Becky, but most of the time that year, I wanted to run alone. Running was my therapy. I was grateful to live by the beach with a town boardwalk. If I couldn't make the whole boardwalk, I would run a couple of blocks. The more I ran, the more I was able to come to terms with my mother's death.

Since my parents never had any money when I was growing up, my mother used to tell me to make a lot of money so that I could support them. As I grew my business, I tried to help as much as I could, but it was never enough. Before my mother died, I told her I would take over my parents' finances. She used to keep a record of everything, but when she got sick, she was unable to. My dad had a severe learning disability and was unable to handle it. His finances were a complete mess. If I didn't run, I don't know how I would have gotten through some of the financial mess I had to get my dad out of.

I felt immense pressure to make sure my dad was okay even though he was never there for me growing up. My mother would have expected me to take care of him. I guess, even after her death, I was still seeking her acceptance.

After the funeral, when my dad returned to Florida, he found one of my mother's mahjong friends and they were like two teenagers in love. After that, my dad pushed everyone away because he found the love of his life. He only called me when he needed me to do something for him. I became his "Girl Friday," tending to his every whim and need.

OCTOBER

As Derek and I went back to Florida to help clean out my dad's apartment and go through all his paperwork, there was a threat that a major hurricane was going to hit Long Beach. No one in town was worried because in the past these types of hurricane threats usually amounted to nothing. Zoey, my daughter, was at school up in Syracuse, New York, at the time.

We didn't prepare. No one did.

Brian stayed in the house when the storm hit. He noticed immediately that water was starting to fill up on our first floor. He knew this was real when he went to use the restroom and saw water gurgling up from the floor. He grabbed the important stuff like our skis, golf clubs, etc., and moved them upstairs.

Everything else downstairs on our first floor was destroyed, including the home gym that we created since I started working out. We had a treadmill, a ski machine, a stationary bike, a universal, a multi-station weight machine, and more. It was the complete package. We had a ton of water damage, and the water was a mixture of sewage and ocean water. The storm practically destroyed our little town. Our boardwalk, which was built in 1907, was also demolished. Pieces of the boardwalk were found blocks away.

When Derek and I returned home, we were lucky enough to rent a car, and decided to drive into Long Beach down the main street to see the damage.

My heart sank yet again. There were boats in the middle of the street! I couldn't believe the storm was that strong. It was devastating. Many of the homes were dismantled, and no one had a car to drive because the salt water from the ocean had ruined them. We had no electricity, and the food in the refrigerator had all gone bad. The Federal Emergency Management Agency (FEMA) was in town. We also had the National Guard there. It was like a war zone.

FEMA provided residents with boxes of food, most of which were in squeeze packets, like the astronauts used in space. It tasted terrible, but it was somewhat nutritious, and we all had to eat it to survive.

Brian, Derek, and I stayed in a Best Western Hotel in Syosset, New York, which was about forty minutes from my home in Lido Beach. Luckily, Lori, secured the hotel for us while we were still in Florida.

Every day, we would clean out a portion of our home. We had some help. Lori, her boyfriend, and Jessica came one day. My friend, Constance, and her husband came another day. Then, Morris came to assist us to take the furniture out onto the street.

The saddest moment was when my mother's electric recliner chair—the one she left in my home to use when she visited—was taken out of my house and thrown in the trash. That was the last bit of my mother, and I was heartbroken.

On Thanksgiving Day, I went to my mother-in-law Marilyn's home. She lived in Long Beach in a beautiful Spanish-style center hall colonial. She invited a couple of her friends from the North Shore to attend the gathering. They experienced a little wind damage from Hurricane Sandy and had the inconvenience of having their lights and cable out, but then came back soon thereafter.

"Did you get hit?" one of the women asked me. I told her my abbreviated version because I didn't want to relive the entire experience.

"Well, it could have been worse . . ." she said.

"Yes, it could have, but it was bad enough," I said and walked away. I didn't want to be rude, but I had heard this saying way too much during the past three weeks, and every time I'd heard it, it had just got me upset.

The next day, I didn't leave my house. Since the first floor was uninhabitable, the upstairs was a disaster with boxes everywhere. I went through the boxes and threw out stuff I really didn't want to keep.

I started with the photo albums. I decided to toss photos I didn't want and to keep the rest in small boxes that I could put up high in my closet so that they wouldn't get destroyed if another storm hit us. It was emotional to look at these photos, all randomly placed in no order as if time were compressed.

That night we had two parties to attend—a fiftieth birthday party for my sister's boyfriend and a sixtieth birthday for a friend. At the first party, my sister's friends came up to me telling me they were sorry for my loss and explaining how lucky they were during the storm. "Nothing happened to our home, and we didn't lose our cars," they told me. "Someone was looking over us."

I was getting frustrated, but I tried to control myself. What? No one was looking over my family and me?

When I went to the second party, which was in my hometown, everyone was depressed. "It's hard to overcome this," said one of my friends, "My business is suffering and it's going to take this town millions of dollars to fix it up."

Another couple stopped me and said, "We were so lucky nothing happened to our home." I smiled and moved on. A friend said her basement got destroyed and in it were photographs of her mother who recently passed away and other family photos. "That was the worst part for me," she confided.

"I've been shuffling around for weeks," another friend told me. "I can't get back in my house."

Someone else told me about the foundation of his home. "Between the house and working fourteen-hour days, it's killing me," he said.

Another friend who had very little damage sat next to me. "Look, it could have been worse," she said. "I know so many people who had their homes burned down and so many people who lost everything. You have to count your blessings."

Yes, it could have been worse, but it didn't make me feel any better. It didn't make this town a happier place. It was a loss for all of us, no matter if we lost a carpet, a car, or our home. It was a loss, and any loss, no matter how big or small, hurts.

After Sandy hit our hometown and destroyed everything, I took a break from running.

I should have continued to run, but my business had taken a downturn again and I was having major staffing problems. My life was a mess.

Lesson Learned

Life is a series of curve balls. Try to go with the flow and if something drastic happens, remember that this is just a moment in time. You will get through it. No one is spared in this world. There are always positives to every negative situation. My positive was that I was safe with my husband and son. Lean on your support system. And if you don't have a support system, seek out help. You will get through it.

2013

"While I'm in heavy training mode, I think there is a burger at the finish and that gets me through!"
–Dereka Hendon-Barnes, Half Ironman, New Jersey

CHAPTER 6

The Year of the Runner

FEBRUARY

After the shock had worn off, a few months following Hurricane Sandy, I reached out to Becky.

"Hey, let's get back into running again," I said.

She was excited. Since we never got to run the Disney Half Marathon, we downloaded an app called 13.1, and we signed up for the Divas Half Marathon in Myrtle Beach.

Every day, we would work on running the length of time that the app said we should. At least once a week, we ran together. The app started with a short run of three minutes and then a walk for two minutes. It continued to provide different walk/run intervals every week until you didn't need to walk.

On the days when I ran alone, it was tough. It was easier to walk instead of run. It was easier to take a little break. It was easier to stop for a while. But when we ran together, we both encouraged each other to go farther.

****

A couple months after starting back up again, I looked outside the window and noticed it was a beautiful sunny day. There were very few clouds in the sky, and it didn't look windy. I put on my outdoor workout gear, along with my sneakers, and went for a short three-mile run. I wasn't sure where I would run. Since our boardwalk was destroyed by Hurricane Sandy, there weren't that many places to safely run in town.

It was windier than I expected. Therefore, I decided to stay close to home. I ran around the neighborhood and noticed that the middle school's gate was broken.

I climbed through the fence and ran toward the track.

There were several different teams there, including the boy's and girl's lacrosse teams and the boy's and the girl's track teams.

I decided to run anyway thinking, "If someone wants me off the track, they will kick me off."

At first, I ran around the track with the girl's track team. Most of the girls seemed to run a quarter mile and were done. I went past the students once, twice, three, and then four times around. On my final lap, I noticed that the boy's track team was right behind me. It was like a herd of cattle. They were running fast and quickly catching up with me.

I got a little nervous, so I cut across the field and went through another broken fence and ran toward the baseball field. I ran around the bases (I always wanted to do that) and ran toward the geese that were hanging out on the field. Surprisingly, they ran faster than me and didn't fly away!

As I headed toward my home, I noticed that my son was riding his bike to the school. I waved.

"Do you need a ride?" I asked.

"Yes," he said.

I told him to ride his bike to the end of the block as I ran. Since I only had a quarter mile left to end my three-mile run, I wanted to finish.

After the run, I walked into the house, got the keys, and drove him to the high school. On our way, he asked me to pull over and pick up his friend, so I did. The friend got into the car and explained how he just came from track practice.

"I was just on the track running," I said.

"Oh, that was you?" he said. "We were all wondering who this random running woman was . . ."

I looked at my son and we laughed.

****

APRIL

The Boston Marathon was the oldest and most prestigious marathon in the country. It always took place on a Monday, which was generally a workday for everyone other than Bostonians. At the Boston Marathon on April 15, 2013, two terrorists planted a bomb that killed three people, injured hundreds of others, and seventeen runners lost limbs as a result.

It struck a chord with me. I was so upset because anyone could have been there. I knew a couple of people running the event and feared for their lives. Thankfully, they were okay, but so many people were killed or injured from the attack. I prayed for the runners and their families. It was so upsetting!

All runners felt anxious, wondering if it would happen again. It was a horrible event that should never have occurred.

RUNNING THE DIVAS HALF MARATHON IN MYRTLE BEACH

When Becky and I arrived in Myrtle Beach, South Carolina, late Friday evening in preparation for our run in the Divas Half Marathon two days later, we were exhausted. We were glad we came in a few days before the event, unlike the Disney Half Marathon.

But we were worried about what happened in Boston. Could it happen here? We tried to shrug off the fear, but it stayed with us.

The next day, we picked up our numbers and walked around the expo. There were about thirty or forty various vendors selling everything from running sneakers to sterling silver running jewelry. Ali Vincent from the first season of *The Biggest Loser* was also there. *The Biggest Loser* was a popular show on television at the time. Contestants who were grossly obese challenged each other to lose weight. The contestant who lost the most weight and didn't get voted out was named the "Biggest Loser."

Becky and I were excited to see her. We were both fans of *The Biggest Loser* since the show's inception.

I asked Ali if she would consider being on my podcast and she agreed. I had started my podcast, *Hilary Topper on Air* in 2011 and was continually building up my base. The podcast helped business owners grow both personally and professionally, and I thought Ali would make a great inspirational guest.

We also got to meet Kendal, the running coach for the Divas Half Marathon & 5K Series. He was especially nice and offered lots of helpful tips on what to do the day before a half marathon, including "don't carb up." He said that if you do, you will have stomach issues during the race.

That evening, we had a light dinner (as suggested by Kendal) and went to bed early.

At 5 a.m., we lined up with the rest of the 5,000 women running the Divas Half Marathon. The organizers gave a moment of silence for the people who lost their lives in the Boston Marathon, then played the national anthem, and we were off.

As I was running the first three miles, I felt as if I were on a huge treadmill. It didn't even feel like I was making any effort. The road just took me.

The Divas folks had water stations after every mile or so. They also organized some of the local radio stations to have live broadcasts on the course. Some of the residents came out to cheer us on. There were so many funny signs along the route. At one point, I was laughing so hard I had to stop! If only I could remember what it said!

There were lots of teams of women and everyone dressed like a "Diva." Becky and I wore tutus and matching outfits.

By mile twelve, I hit the wall. I really didn't think I could keep going. We ran along Route 17 and there were still cars coming next to us. At one point, one of the runners screamed as a truck went by. This threw me off. I panicked. "Come on Hilary," Becky said. "You have to keep going. Don't stop!"

To be honest, toward the end of the race, I was starting to get mad at Becky because I really needed to walk, and she refused.

At the last quarter mile there were dozens of people, which motivated us to sprint to the finish line. We finished the race in under three hours.

After the Divas Half Marathon, Becky and I ran several local races. We also decided to sign up for the Disney Tower of Terror Race in September. We needed to get in at least one Disney race!

JULY

By the summer, I heard that a part of the new Long Beach Boardwalk was up. I decided to run from my house in Lido to the Long Beach boardwalk, which started on Long Beach Road and spanned four blocks west. The run was a little difficult since it was extremely hot and running in the middle of the street with cars coming is not the most pleasant experience. But I was determined.

Since the Divas Half Marathon, I hadn't run more than a couple of miles a day. I just couldn't get myself back into the long runs. But I decided to go for it.

When I finally came to Long Beach Road, I walked up the ramp and I saw dozens of smiling people. It was a gorgeous day, with a bright blue sky, and scattered fluffy white clouds. The sun illuminated everything, so the colors were intensified. It felt good to see happy people again. It had been too long.

Hurricane Sandy destroyed our 2.1-mile boardwalk. Since then, we had had nothing there. In addition to many folks being displaced, the boardwalk was the heart and soul of our city. Seeing it gone was tragic for all of us. Until now . . .

I ran the four blocks on the new boardwalk. It wasn't rickety like the old one. There weren't loose boards either. It was straight, flat, and bouncy. Boy, was it bouncy! I had been running on asphalt for way too long. Running on the boardwalk felt as if I were on a trampoline. It was wonderful.

Although it was fast and short, it made me feel hopeful that there would be a new 2.1-mile boardwalk soon and then us runners—and there were plenty of us living in Long Beach—could get back to running on the boardwalk again.

GETTING HOOKED

I started getting hooked on running again. If I were traveling for work, I would see if there was a race in the area. If I were going on vacation, I would try to explore the area through running. I loved to run.

It helped me sort out things that were troubling me, and it made me feel happy.

During my travels, I ran along Lake Shore Drive in Chicago, on a dirt path in Sanibel, Florida, on Lady Bird Trail in Austin, Texas, and on a rail trail in Bermuda. If there was a trail, I was there.

Lesson Learned

Sometimes it's good to be pushed by a friend or by yourself. If you think that you don't want to "kill yourself" when you work out or do anything endurance related, it's the wrong mindset. Being pushed or pushing yourself won't hurt. It may even help get you faster!

CHAPTER 7

Becoming Obsessed With Jeff Galloway

OCTOBER

There were more than 10,000 people registered for Disney's Tower of Terror Run in Orlando, and Becky and I were two of them.

We arrived in Orlando on Friday and headed over to the Disney Expo where we walked around and met various vendors selling running-related gear. We also had the opportunity to attend two workshops—one on what to expect during the race and one with Jeff Galloway, an Olympic athlete who was the *run*Disney training consultant.

Jeff was a thin man who was very kind. He spent time talking with all his fans. He was the author of many books, and he seemed knowledgeable.

After talking with him, Becky and I sat and listened with the rest of the audience as Jeff Galloway mesmerized us with his knowledge of the sport. He was an incredible speaker and had so much worthwhile information to share.

Galloway spoke about his Run Walk Run method. He explained how this method helped prevent injuries and got you to your goal faster because there were adequate rest periods in between your run.

"Do you think we can do that?" I asked Becky.

She looked at me and said, "Let's try it out for this race."

After his talk, we both hurried to the Galloway booth, bought two of his books, his timer, and I asked Jeff to sign our books. We even got the opportunity to take a photo with him. I felt as if I met a celebrity.

"Will you be on my podcast?" I asked him. He agreed. OMG, I was so excited!

We went back to the room, and I quickly looked through the book to see if there were any helpful tips to get us through the race.

The next day we waited for the race to begin. Becky said she felt as if we waited all day, which we did. The race didn't start until 10 p.m.

At around 7 p.m., after putting on our running gear and dressing up as "evil fairies," we caught the bus to MGM Studios with dozens of other runners. We weren't the only ones dressed up. When we got to the start of the race, everyone was there, including Snow White, Minnie Mouse, fairy princesses, Batman, Wonder Woman, skeletons, and more. You name it; there was someone dressed as every character!

We had a few hours of sitting around, stretching out before being shuffled to the corrals. We were in corral G.

The corrals started moving. First, the wheelchair racers, then the elite runners took off. It was slow going but it moved. As each corral took off, the race directors played the theme song to *The Twilight Zone*, then there were fireworks, and it looked as if the runners were running into a time warp. There were laser lights that illuminated the sky and created the illusion that you were running into the abyss.

There were plenty of Disney villains out on the route including Captain Hook, Scar from *The Lion King*, and the queen from *Alice in Wonderland*. Many people stopped and took photos with their favorite villains, but we just kept running. Let me tell you, these Disney races were no joke. They were hard!

We tried out Jeff Galloway's Run Walk Run method. We ran two minutes and then walked for one minute, as suggested in one of his original books. His later books suggest thirty seconds or less of a walk break. We did stop at the water stations because the humidity was deadly. It was hot, even at 11 p.m.!

The thing about Jeff Galloway's method, we never hit the wall. We could have easily done another three miles to finish a half marathon.

One of the highlights was when we ran through MGM Studios' backlots. It felt as if we were running a block in Manhattan. We also enjoyed running around the track because the concrete was so hard on the bottom of our feet, especially since, at that time, we were wearing barefoot sneakers.

I felt excited to start learning a new way to run, race at *run*Disney, and share the experience with Becky!

A few weeks after I got back, my CFO hit me with some bad business news. She told me that our bank account had dwindled, and, with the loss of some big clients, we needed to make some major cuts. Talk about stress. We had just finished producing *Glasslandia*, the first Google Glass reality show on YouTube. I was one of the original Google Glass Explorers. (Google Glass was a smart headset that connected to the Internet.) We had spent a fortune to produce the series, and I wished I had saved the money!

My business went from being so incredible to so devastating. I couldn't cut staff. I loved these people so much. So, I cut almost everything else, including my salary, and we moved out of Melville and back to a lower overhead space in Long Beach.

At first it was depressing, and we all found it difficult to work. Slowly, I lost more staff and I decided to reinvent my business.

In the meantime, running was my only outlet. If I didn't run, I don't know how I would have handled that downturn.

Lesson Learned

Running is a fantastic way to relieve stress. If you've never run or you have had multiple injuries, the Run Walk Run method is worth giving a try. Once you are into it, you may want to go on trips and run in interesting and unique places. I hope you get the opportunity to do that on your travels. I know you will love it!

2014

"Swimming is my nemesis, so, I think about Dory the fish and at the start of every race, I think 'Just keep swimming.' For whatever reason, all the nervousness falls away several minutes into the swim. I breathe and count my strokes and eventually I calm down. And I just keep swimming."

–Jacqueline Brown, Ironman, Michigan

CHAPTER 8

Brooklyn Half Marathon

During the first few months of the year, my business was status quo—things weren't improving, but they weren't bad either. We picked up a couple of new clients, so we were moving in a forward direction.

In March, at a networking party, I saw a colleague of mine and asked if he needed adjunct professors for his new Master's in Public Relations program at Hofstra University, a private school on Long Island. After a series of interviews, I was asked to teach, and I absolutely loved the experience. It was something different. It gave me an opportunity to mentor many students, which I loved. I continued to run and enjoyed life again. Things were good.

Becky and I were still training and were thrilled to see that Team for Kids had a couple of slots left to run the Brooklyn Half Marathon. We fundraised, and that May, we were ready.

MAY

At 5:45 a.m. on Saturday, May 16, the day of the race, Becky's van was in front of my house. Her husband was driving. I jumped in and started to organize myself. I was nervous. I couldn't sleep the night before. I kept dreaming of missing the race.

We stopped for coffee on our way. When I got back into their van, I banged my head so hard that it knocked me down to the ground. My head was throbbing. I kept thinking this is it. We're not going to run this race now.

But I shook myself off and climbed back into the van. We were on our way.

Becky's husband drove us close as possible to Grand Army Plaza in Brooklyn, New York—the start of the race. When he couldn't go any farther because of the police barricades, Becky and I got out of the van and walked about a mile to the corral.

We met some interesting people at the corral, including a "pacer." She was pacing at 2:30. This was the first race that we noticed pacers. They generally help you keep within a specific time, for example, the 2:30 pacer will help the group finish at exactly two hours and thirty minutes.

"Let's try to keep up with her," Becky said to me.

I was reluctant. We had both been running slower than an eleven-minute mile, and I didn't want to go out too hard or too fast in the beginning, but I said, okay.

Once we were off, we stayed with the pacer and the group for about two miles and then I couldn't keep the pace. Becky slowed down. "You can stay with them, if you want," I told her. But she didn't want to.

The first couple of miles were difficult. The backs of my legs hurt, and all I wanted to do was shake the pain away, but I didn't want to stop. Becky and I walked through the water stations and ran the rest of the time.

On mile five, Becky told me her back was hurting badly. "Do you want to stop?" I asked her. She looked at me and said, "You know me better than that. Once I start something, I have to finish!" So, we continued.

The first seven miles were in and around Prospect Park. When we left the park, we got a boost of energy. "Here we are Brooklyn," I shouted. "Coney Island here we come!"

"I guess we're on track since we're not being taken off the course," I said. We gave each other a high five.

Most races have a time limit due to road closures or park closures. The time limits are different at every race. The Brooklyn Half Marathon had a 3:15-minute time limit. If you didn't reach a certain point, you were "swept" away (or picked up by a shuttle). Having these time limits made the races much more stressful, especially for someone like me who was a back-of-the-packer.

It was exciting to leave the park and go on Ocean Parkway. We went down the ramp to get on the parkway and then continued to Coney Island.

At mile twelve, I was feeling pretty good. I wasn't hurting, well, maybe a little. We stopped at the fluid station, had a drink, and ran. One mile to the finish line. In the distance, I could see Coney Island and the boardwalk. My heart was racing. "This is it," I said to Becky, "we're almost there!"

As we got closer to the boardwalk, we passed the New York Aquarium. We passed the Cyclone. We went up on the boardwalk. We both had another boost of energy and sprinted to the finish line. As we passed the finish line, we both got emotional. We felt like crying. It was an amazing feeling to get there after training for so many months! We got our medals, had our photo taken, and got a bagel to munch on.

Both Becky and I ran our fastest half marathon to date. I was thrilled I didn't hit the wall at mile twelve, and I also had a personal record (PR).

Reflecting on this experience, I realize that I had a PR because we were running a lot. Becky and I were both running at least three days a week with the long run on the weekends, and that helped us.

After that race, Becky told me she was done. "What do you mean?" I asked. "I don't want to run any long running races anymore," she said.

I was disappointed but said, "Why don't we do a triathlon?" I had heard about a triathlon, which is a swim, bike, and run in one event, in Sanibel by the Beaches of Fort Myers/Sanibel when I was recruited to take part in a Google Glass exploration. With four other Explorers, I was asked to take photos and videos using Glass. While there, I was told about the Captiva Tri. I loved the area so much I thought it would be awesome to do a triathlon in such a beautiful place.

Lesson Learned

If you want to go faster, be consistent. Make sure to run three to four days a week. I promise you will see a difference.

CHAPTER 9

We Signed Up for a Triathlon!

APRIL

Becky and I signed up for the Captiva Tri in September. But we didn't realize what we were getting ourselves into! It sounded like a cool idea, but what did it entail?

"We need to find a coach," Becky said to me.

"Why?" I asked, "We never needed a coach for any of our other events."

"I'm telling you, we need to hire a coach," she said.

And with that, I called Constance and asked her if she would coach us. Constance was one of the fittest people I knew and a marketer I met during my tenure with Social Media Association, a group that I started. She was on my Board of Directors. She had lots of posts about triathlons on social media, and I looked up to her. Constance was doing an Ironman that summer, and I thought she would be perfect to help get us through the training for a sprint triathlon, which was a quarter-mile swim, ten-mile bike ride, and a 5K run. She said she was honored that we asked her, "But I think you should call my coach, Richie. He is great and I know you will love him."

Constance got Richie on the phone. I told him my goal was to be able to get through the race. "I'm not looking to win. I just want to complete it." (Again, I didn't want to push myself.)

He was great. I loved his enthusiasm for the sport and his raw, honest feedback. He told me that getting involved in triathlon was not an inexpensive endeavor.

"You need a good carbon fiber road bike, helmet, and lots of other gear," he said. "And once you get the bike, don't think that you'll be able to get on and just ride. It's a bit of a transition when you wear riding shoes that clip into the pedals."

I got off the phone and was nervous. I told Becky to call him, too. She did but she wanted to work with a coach who lived closer to the south shore of Long Island. "He's way too far away," she said.

Richie lived out in Suffolk County, which was about an hour or so from my home. Since I was used to virtual trainers, it didn't matter to me where he was located.

So, Becky went with a local coach, and I decided to train with Richie and his team. "Look, we're not going to be able to stay together anyway during this triathlon, so it doesn't really matter which coach we both go with. And anyway, we'll be able to compare notes," Becky said.

****

Before deciding on hiring a coach, Becky and I signed up to swim at the Long Beach Recreation Center. We knew we needed to start there.

My first step was to buy a bathing cap. Yes, I didn't have one because I hadn't gone swimming in decades! And anyway, who wears bathing caps?

That first day in the pool was a mess. I doggy-paddled across the length of the pool and was exhausted. On the way back I did a Tarzan—a freestyle swim without putting my face in the water. I didn't know I was doing a Tarzan. I didn't even know it was called something. I just didn't want my face in the water. It took forever to get across the pool. I kept stopping along the way. It was horrible.

"I think you have to put your face in the water," Becky told me.

"Urgh . . ." I said. At that, a lifeguard walked over to us. "Where are your goggles?" she asked me.

"I don't have a pair," I said.

She walked over and picked up an extra pair by the lifeguard chair. "Here, wear these," she said.

I tried putting my face in the water, but after a couple of strokes I kept choking on the water. I even threw up! How am I going to swim 400 yards if I can't swim one length of the pool—just twenty-five yards?

After a lap in the pool, my heart was racing so hard I could feel it in my face! But I wasn't going to give up.

My whole life, people told me I couldn't do this, or I couldn't do that. When people said that to me it motivated me even further to prove them wrong!

Next step was to buy a bicycle.

Richie suggested two starter bikes for me—the Trek Domane and the Felt ZW4. I did my homework and learned that although the bike is important the components are just as important, if not more important.

Brian went with me to a local bike shop. "Let's see what they have and then make a decision," he said. Although, my new coach didn't encourage it, we went to the shop anyway and met up with a young man who seemed very knowledgeable about road bikes. I rode six bikes, including Trek and Cannondale.

"Wow, what a ride," I said, when I got off the Trek Domane. The bike was black and white with green accents. It was a beauty. I didn't buy it at the bike store because it wasn't the bike store that my coach recommended. I'm not sure why I felt compelled to listen to everything he said, but I did.

The salesperson said that the price was negotiable and that he would get me a great deal especially if I were to buy other things in the store.

Since Richie and Constance had highly recommended that I go to a bike store about forty minutes away, I wanted to go there.

We met the owner at the Manhasset location. He was very helpful. He had brought an aluminum bike over from the Great Neck store. I tried that bike and really enjoyed the ride.

Then he showed me the carbon fiber bikes he had. They were a bit more expensive than the aluminum-framed bikes, but they really were lighter and seemed more efficient, even riding around the busy parking lot behind his shop.

I rode another Cannondale, Felt Z3 (which is slighter lower end than Richie had suggested), and two Trek Silques (which were the new versions of the Domane). I really enjoyed the higher-end one, but it was way out of my budget, so I decided against it. I ended up going with the bike that was the one step down. The bike was teal blue with a white seat and white handlebars. It looked hot!

My anxiety started to resonate when the owner said you will need this, this, and that. The next thing I knew, I was spending a few hundred more on stuff to go with the bike—the pedals, the bag to carry the tools in case you get a flat, the helmet, the gloves, the bike shorts, etc.

OMG, what have I gotten myself into?

Lesson Learned

Trying anything new in life is scary, exciting, and exhilarating. I listened to my coach and went out and spent thousands of dollars. But you don't have to do that. If you want to try doing a triathlon, go with what you have or borrow something at first. Later, if you like the sport, buy the fancy gear that goes with it.

CHAPTER 10

My First Training Week

MAY

My checklist:

- Hired Coach Richie and joined a triathlon team
- Bought a road bike
- Bought a Garmin 910xt watch
- Bought swimsuits and nose plugs (Side note: The plastic ones were no good. They kept slipping off.)
- Bought riding shorts to soften my ride
- Hired a swim instructor
- Signed up for a Master Swim Team.

Okay, everything was checked off my list and I was ready for training week 1. Coach Richie sent me a schedule on TrainingPeaks, an online scheduler that provided customized training activities for the week. He prepared it, which was different than the Virtual Trainer that I used for both the NYC Half and the Brooklyn Half. (The Virtual Trainer was specifically for running half or full marathons and integrated your time into an algorithm that calculated your training program. It was a proprietary program from New York Road Runners.)

My first week consisted of two rest days (Yay!), two days of swimming combined with either running or biking, and two days of running and biking alone with the long ride and run on the weekends.

Not being able to swim made the swim portion daunting. Coach Richie wanted me to do 1,600 yards of swimming or sixty-four laps. I could barely do twenty-five yards, which is just one lap! Really? How am I going to do that?

The bike portion was difficult, too. Using riding shoes and clipping in and out was challenging. I fell several times (well, actually a dozen times!) with and without the clips. Getting on and off a bike was always difficult for me.

Even the run portion seemed intimidating. I found it nearly impossible to run a mile! (Did I lose it since the half marathons?)

I felt discouraged the first week. I questioned myself a lot. Why am I doing this? But then I shook my head and thought, I'm going to do this. I need to prove to myself that I can do anything I set my mind to do. I've done it in business, I can do it with a triathlon too!

Although I was always picked last in school gym class, it doesn't mean that as an adult I won't be good at something. I played golf and I was okay at that, I thought.

And besides when my grandfather told me to "shoot for the stars," it resonated with me. It didn't matter that my parents had no money, and we couldn't get things like the rest of the kids in the school. If I wanted something, I could accomplish it myself.

I was proud of myself for getting up at 5:30 a.m. to get the workouts done, even if I didn't feel like it. I knew that I was doing something good for myself, both physically and mentally, and decided to push forward.

Later that week, Lisa, from my office, was in for the week. She lived in Colorado and was staying with me because we had client meetings. So, I brought her along with me to meet Coach Richie and my new swim coach, Bryan Krut of Open Water Swim LI.

The Open Water Swim LI folks told me to go to the first lane and start there. I don't think I ever swallowed so much water in my entire life as I did during that swim. It also kept going up my nose. For some reason, I find it nearly impossible to breathe out of my nose in the water. After a series of drills, I found myself burping up chlorine and I started to dry heave in the pool.

The next time I went to the training, Bryan jumped in the water with me as I was struggling and taught me how to blow bubbles. He sat there for a while making me put my face in the water and blow.

Now, I really had to stick my face in the water!

Christine, another coach, worked with me too, so that I was able to easily get across the pool and swim twenty-five yards. I couldn't believe I could do it. What an accomplishment to swim twenty-five yards without choking or throwing up!

RIDING

The next day, I wanted to wake up at 5:30 a.m. but my alarm never went off, so I woke up at 6:30 a.m. instead. Since I had to make sure my son got to school, I had to wait another hour or so before I could go for my forty-five-minute ride.

At 8 a.m., I got on my new Trek Silque bike with my clips and started to ride. (If you could call it that . . .)

It was raining. I had asked my coach about that, and he said that people ride in the rain. I realized that I didn't have my wallet, my mobile phone, or any other piece of ID. I didn't have my riding gloves either. I remembered the guy from the bike shop saying to me that if I fall, the gloves will protect my hands. Well, I better not fall.

I rode cautiously to the boardwalk. There was a lot of traffic. I got on the boardwalk and thought I would be alone, but there were still plenty of other people out there running, cycling, or just walking in the rain.

I went for fifteen minutes at a moderate pace. The next fifteen minutes I went faster. My heart rate went up to 140+. The wind was blowing against me, and it felt nearly impossible to pedal. I pushed through. I kept thinking about what Constance told me, "Just get through it."

The wind was shaking the bike. I was feeling unstable. I slowed down, but I forgot about the clips and went down. The bike fell on top of me, and my feet were still clipped in. A little old man with a cane came running over to me, "Are you alright?" he asked.

"Yes, thank you. The wind was so strong it took me down," I said. He didn't answer. He just walked away.

I got back on the bike and rode home. I smiled to myself. I "got it done."

Lesson Learned

When you start out, focus internally. Don't look at the other athletes in the pool, on the track, or riding around you. Just stay focused on you. Stay strong. If people want to help, accept it; everyone remembers their first time, and they are happy to help a newbie!

CHAPTER 11

First Training Weekend

JUNE

The weekend started with a bike ride along the Wantagh State Parkway with my husband. He was a much stronger rider than I was. He led. It was hard to keep up. We rode over two narrow bridges, which scared me especially since other cyclists were coming in the opposite direction.

Once we got over the third bridge, we came to the end and rode through the Jones Beach parking lot to the Tobay bike path. This was the trickiest part of the loop because there were lots of directional cones that were rather confusing. It felt as if I were riding my bicycle through an obstacle course.

As we followed the cones past Zach's Bay, we rode up an incline that led us to the Tobay path. We didn't ride the whole path, which at that point was only seventeen miles. We rode twelve miles, and it felt good until we got off the bike. Then, my legs were shaking.

HILL REPEATS

My coach called for hill repeats or trail running the following day. The only hill I could think of was the Norman J Levy Park & Preserve in South Merrick. The trail wasn't that long, only about three miles roundtrip.

I started out strong. I ate an energy gel and ran a fast twelve-minute mile (well, fast for me). The second mile was tough. It felt as if it were straight uphill. I was tired and hot. That mile went a lot slower. I reached the top of the hill and thought about taking a "selfie" and saying I'm on top of the world, the south shore world. But I didn't. I looked at the view and smiled. I made it. I could do this . . .

****

I felt pretty good after the run, and that same day, I thought about going to the pool at the Long Beach Recreation Center. Becky and I joined about a month before, which gave us unlimited access to the pool and the weight room. I did a bunch of errands around the house and then decided to head over to practice breathing in the water. I was still having some trouble, but with the help of Bryan, I started to feel as if I could get it, especially with his suggestion to get nose plugs. I felt a little silly wearing them, but they worked!

I wanted to practice. If I could not do something, I became determined to learn how. I also knew I needed to get in the open water because the sprint triathlon we signed up for was in the Gulf of Mexico. Bryan told me I needed to get myself a wetsuit.

He said when you're in trouble in the water, all you do is float on your back. Hmm, I liked that. It made me feel more relaxed swimming in the open water. I hadn't been in the open water since I was a kid at summer camp, and, even then, I didn't really swim. I learned the side stroke. Does that count? Will this be the same experience?

BUYING MY FIRST WETSUIT

I called Constance for advice. "What do you think? Should I swim in open water?" I asked her.

"Of course, you should," she said. "But first thing, we need to get you a wetsuit." I agreed and we set a date.

A few days later, Constance and I met at the Runner's Edge in Farmingdale. A young woman asked what we were looking for. We told her and she came back with a wetsuit. I struggled and struggled to get it on. I worked up a total sweat. I did speed training around the track in the morning, and I was sweating more putting on the wetsuit. It didn't have the greatest fit.

"It will be fine for a rental," the young woman told us.

"Oh no, you have it wrong," said Constance. "We are looking to buy a wetsuit."

"Oh, in that case, let me bring out some things for you to try on," the salesperson said.

I looked at Constance. She knew what I was thinking. She smiled and laughed.

The next suit was a TYR suit. "This is the less expensive version," the salesperson said. I took the other one off quickly and proceeded to put on the first TYR suit. I got one leg in. I was breathing heavy. The sweat was dripping off my face. I got another leg in and proceeded to pull it up. I started to jump up and down to get the crotch to come up as it was drooping.

I started having visions of my mother and grandmother trying to get on a girdle back in the 1970s. My mother would jump up and down to get it on. I was finding myself doing the same thing with this TYR wetsuit. After about fifteen minutes or longer, I finally got it on. Constance helped me zip it up, and I noticed that the neck didn't fit right. It was loose.

Another salesperson came by and tightened it up, but it still didn't fit right. At this point, the sweat was now dripping off my entire body as if it were a ninety-degree day.

From Couch Potato to Endurance Athlete

"You should try on the other suit," Constance said. I pulled the suit off so quickly. I couldn't wait to get it off. Now on to suit three. I kept thinking, I was a ball of sweat, my heart was racing so fast, how would I ever get this on? The last suit felt like it took hours to put on!

The second TYR was a better version of the first and more expensive. I didn't realize that wetsuits were so expensive! They were nearly $1,000 each. Boy, when Coach Richie said this sport was not for the "cheap at heart," he was right. It was an expensive sport!

I pulled up one leg at a time and, again, had issues with the crotch. I jumped and jumped and jumped. "It's coming," said Constance.

Now I was making a scene. I felt as though the whole store was watching. One of the managers came over and helped me get it on. FINALLY!

One sleeve was longer than the other, but he felt that the fit was perfect. I looked at Constance and the salesperson. They shook their heads in agreement. I guess this is the one I'm going to buy. I carried the wetsuit up to the front desk. The woman started to ring me up and I said, "Now I just hope I can get this on."

"Oh, here you go," she said and handed me some glide to use prior to putting on the wetsuit. "Use this around your neck, wrists, and ankles and you'll get it on. And this is our gift to you."

Hmm, why didn't she give this to me earlier? Now, let's see if I can get the wetsuit back on when I finally go out for an open water swim.

Lesson Learned

Go outside your comfort zone. You will find a whole new world out there! Don't forget to laugh at yourself. Just have fun and smile when you can.

CHAPTER 12

Triathlon Firsts

MY FIRST BRICK

I got a call from Constance asking me if I was going to do the brick over the weekend. "I hadn't heard about it," I told her. She said, "You will."

Later that day, my coach called and told me the tri team was going to do a brick workout together.

"Ummm, brick?" I said, "Could you explain?"

He told me a brick is a workout you build upon utilizing two or three different disciplines, like placing one brick on top of another.

"We will swim in the Long Island Sound, bike around Mount Sinai and Port Jefferson, and then run around the beach park," he said.

I was in. I didn't know what to expect and was anxious all week thinking about this workout and whether I could do it. I knew the rest of the team were experienced triathletes, with many training for an Ironman or training for an Olympic triathlon. But I decided to go for it anyway.

Friday night, I set my alarm for 4 a.m. I had all my stuff set:

- For swimming—bathing suit, goggles, nose plugs, a towel, and my wetsuit
- For biking—biking shorts, jersey, sports bra, compression socks, clip on riding shoes, helmet, riding gloves, water bottles, and sunscreen
- For running—running shorts, running top, sneakers, Team for Kids hat, water belt, headphones, and gel.

I threw on some clothes, packed the car, put the bike on the rack, and set the GPS for the North Shore of Long Island. I put on my favorite music station, Alt Nation, and was on my way. It took me well over an hour to head northeast.

I got to Cedar Beach in Mount Sinai at 5:40 a.m. Richie was already there with another teammate, Eric. "I don't think you should swim today," Richie told me. "It's really rough and there are no lifeguards on duty."

I sat and waited until the rest of the team got there. No one wanted to go in the water, but since it was so close for so many of them to do their Ironman races, Richie insisted they go in. Richie was a yeller. He motivated people by telling them how he felt. He kind of reminded me of my mother. He used negative reinforcement, but when you did something good, he commended you and that felt real because you didn't get it often.

I watched as everyone put on their wetsuits, jumped in the water, and were tumbled around as though in a giant washing machine. Since I just started swimming a few weeks ago, I was glad that Richie told me to stay out.

About an hour later, everyone came out and started to change for the bike part of the brick. I noticed that Richie and Eric had a tri kit on with the team's name. Interestingly, they used the same suit, although it was wet, for the bike and run portion of the brick. I always wondered about the changing part in a triathlon. By wearing one suit, it cut out a lot of the "transition time" between one activity to the next.

"Are you going to bike in that wet one-piece suit?" I asked Eric. He nodded his head, yes.

I was all changed and ready to go on the bike tour. I wasn't sure where I was going but I assumed there were signs along the route.

Richie told me to start. "Don't worry," he said, "we will catch up."

I headed out of the parking lot, along a road that followed around a boat basin. Hills surrounded the alcove and I continued to head straight uphill. I shifted my gear. Since I was also very new to riding a bike,

I was uncertain about the gears, but I kept clicking until I felt like I could make it up the hill.

I rode for a while and wasn't sure if I turned at the right spot. At one point, I got off the bike and stood there waiting for someone to come by. I saw two joggers and asked where 25A was. They pointed me in a direction of a huge hill. Another walker I asked pointed me in a different direction. I wasn't sure where to go. I remembered Richie telling me left, right, left, but since I'm directionally challenged, I wasn't sure where I was supposed to turn.

Suddenly, a swarm of cyclists flew past me. It was the tri team. I was on the wrong side of the street and by the time I turned around, they were gone. I noticed a few stragglers who passed me as I was turning. Constance was one of them, "You got this Hilary. You can do it!" she said.

I finally got to 25A but started to panic. I really didn't know where I was. I wasn't sure how far out to go. I wasn't 100% confident on the bike. So, I turned around and headed back. I thought I knew how to get back to the car and I did.

Once there, I put the bike on the rack and quickly changed. I took a short run through the beach park. It was a magnificent view. I saw amazing houses on the hills overlooking the water. I ran up and down a dock and even passed a deer. I didn't even know there were deer on Long Island!

When I finished, I got into my car and decided not to wait for the rest of the group. Most of them were riding 100 miles and then running at least a 10K. I headed home.

I wasn't feeling good about my performance. I was upset about the whole thing. I started having flashbacks about being the last picked in gym class. "I am such a loser!" I thought to myself.

Now this part may sound a little crazy, but I started to give myself a pep talk. Here's what went right:

- I got up early.
- I did my first brick workout.

- This whole sport is totally new to me, and I have been pushing myself to do it, and I am doing it. I may not be the fastest, but at least I was out there getting it done.

But my pep talk didn't last. I got down on myself. I started to tell myself that I couldn't do anything right.

Later in the day, I got a call from Constance. "Hey, you did it," she said encouraging me. She made me feel better.

Richie had me off for two days, but I wasn't ready to take two days off. I felt I needed more practice on the bike. So, the next morning, I woke up, packed up the car, and took the bike over to the Wantagh State Parkway. I decided to ride the new route to Tobay Beach. I road 8.5 miles there and 8.5 miles back, completing my first seventeen-mile bike ride!

I texted Richie—"Now that I rode seventeen miles, I feel I deserve to take a day off." He wrote back, "Good job."

I felt happy and rode home.

BIKE DILEMMA

Learning to swim, bike, and run was a huge challenge for me. I never thought that it would have been this difficult to do a triathlon. No one tells you how hard it really is!

When I saw the post about an upcoming Captiva Tri, I thought this could be something different. It didn't sound that hard. I never thought that I would have to hire a coach and learn a whole new way of working out!

For example, more than eight weeks ago, I didn't even get into a pool, let alone swim! Ask anyone; I didn't like to be in the water. So, learning how to swim the right way was my first challenge.

The bike was another challenge. I had to relearn to ride a bike. "Hil, let's face it, you never really were a good rider," said Brian.

I got on the bike. It took a few moments to propel myself forward. Then, once I was riding, I was okay. And shifting? What the heck was that? I grew up in Long Beach. There were no hills there. It was flat as a pancake. I used one gear. That's all I ever needed.

The other day, I had to stop before going over a bridge. I started to cramp up and psyched myself out of the climb. It took several minutes before I could get myself back on the bike.

There was so much to think about—the gears, the cadence (the amount of time the wheels turn over), the clips (clipping on and off), the position of my hands. I didn't want to take them off the brakes. I was also a little nervous about standing up. You know what, the bike makes me nervous!

I read an article in a bicycle magazine that said a lot of people had bike anxiety, and the way to get rid of it is to focus on the moment. I tried that, but when I was also trying to focus on cadence, heart rate, and speed, it made it difficult.

Don't get me wrong, I loved the feeling of being on a bike. It was an amazing feeling to ride.

But I had so much anxiety.

One day soon after, I was walking in New York City with a junior associate from my public relations firm, and we were talking about riding the bicycle and my fear, when suddenly, we saw a man on his bicycle get hit by a Smart Car. The man went flying in the air.

It was so disturbing. The cyclist picked himself up and went on his way, but my employee and I were startled.

"Do you think this means something?" I said to her.

I reached out to my coach. "I've been hit by a car three times and the head coach was hit five times," he told me. Hmm, is that supposed to make me feel better?

Maybe I was supposed to see that. Maybe my message was it happens, and you move on. Not sure, but I know one thing, I needed to build up my confidence on the bike otherwise I wouldn't be able to get this done.

TEN WEEKS LATER . . .

I started training for the Captiva Tri in June. At first, I wasn't sure about the sport. I never swam nor biked much. I knew one thing—I loved to run.

Once I hired a coach, I was still unsure. Is this something I like?

It was a lot of money to get started. Before I knew it, I was spending thousands of dollars on a sport I didn't even know if I would enjoy. I started training five days a week, which turned into six. It quickly became habit forming and an addiction.

Now, I was obsessed! (Have a good workout? I hope so!)

All I wanted to talk about was swimming, cycling, and running. I was driving my family crazy, including my husband who ignored me!

I started reading articles on gear and looking for local events in my area. And, whenever someone talked about triathlons or Ironman, all I wanted to do was find out more!

I loved running, but I was never this obsessed. I'm finding the swimming like running. You get into a rhythm, and you don't want to stop. You feel like you can keep going forever. All three sports help you feel free. I needed that feeling, especially since I always felt trapped in my past. I needed to clean it away and make a fresh start.

MY FIRST TIME IN OPEN WATER

My first experience in the open water was not fun. I met up with a group from Open Water Swim LI at Robert Moses State Park. Even with the Body Glide, I struggled to get on my wetsuit. Then, I inched my way into the murky water. There was so much seaweed there, and the water was so incredibly mucky. I had a hard time getting in.

Bryan saw me struggling. He pulled up to me on a jet ski and told me to climb aboard. "I'll take you out a little further to get you away from the muck," he said.

I attempted to swim but couldn't get more than a few yards. Bryan was very helpful. He told me to try doing drills in the water and encouraged me to spot a location so that I could see where I was going. He called that spotting. He tried to calm me down and told me I was doing great for the first time, but I was still discouraged.

My second time was at Tobay Beach. I signed up for the Aqua Run and then realized I couldn't do the event because my Captiva Tri was the same day. In preparation for the event, the organizers had an open water swim. I decided to go over and check it out.

The water at Tobay was much calmer than the water at Robert Moses. I also found that getting on my wetsuit was a little easier than the first time. But I was slow to get it on, and by the time I reached the water, the other participants were finished with the swim. The organizers for the Aqua Run had three police boats out and two people on kayaks in case anyone was in trouble.

I walked out into the water. "How are you doing?" one of the men on the kayaks asked me.

"Well, this is my first time in the open water," I lied. Even though it was my second, it was my first time at Tobay Beach. "I'm a little nervous."

He stayed with me. Then another swimmer saw me and stayed with me too. I was swimming in Tobay Beach with a stranger and a kayaker who encouraged me to keep going. The whole fleet stayed with me until I finished. When I got to the beach, they all came off and gave me a high five. I was a little embarrassed. But I got a private lesson!

My third time was when I went to Florida to see my dad and brother's family. My husband, children, and I stayed at the Marriott at Pompano Beach. It was a nice resort with a beautiful beach.

The first day I went out and the water was calm, like a lake. I swam with no problem. My husband and children were cheering me on.

My family had never seen me in the water. I used to go in, dunk, and come out. They were surprised at how long I was in the ocean.

"Wow, Mom, you're doing so good. You have great form," Zoey said to me. Both Zoey and Derek have been so encouraging throughout this entire journey.

"She's right," said my son, "Dad and I can't keep up with you!"

It made me smile. I had only been swimming for ten weeks, and all that hard work was finally paying off!

The next three days, I made it my business to go out and swim back and forth between the buoys. They were rough days. It was nothing like the first day. The waves were big and crashed against me as I swam. The tide pulled me out and I had to fight the current. It was great practice.

I got myself into a rhythm.

I was pleased with my performance and felt that maybe I was getting the hang of it.

TRANSITION PRACTICE

If someone asked me a year ago, what it takes to be a triathlete, I would have said, "Hmm . . . someone who could swim, bike, and run?"

What I didn't realize is, there are two other disciplines to master— proper nutrition/hydration and transitions. Both seem simple on the surface but are quite complicated.

I thought water and a couple of gels were fine, but Richie told me to get an electrolyte mix for my water. "Don't go out without putting something in the water," he said. Constance suggested a particular hydration mix. I tried it and used it for every training, along with gels, if the workout was longer than an hour.

Since I started training for the Captiva Tri, I didn't really think much about transitions, but I knew they were important.

The faster you get out of T1 (that's the first transition area from swim to bike,) and then T2 (bike to run), the better you will do with your overall time. As you get better at this sport, seconds count. So, this is one of the important areas to focus on during training.

Richie put up a post on Facebook, "Anyone interested in a transition clinic? I'm having one at my house on Saturday."

I told him I was in, and on Saturday, I left ample time and headed out an hour east to his home.

I met up with five other teammates also interested in getting faster during transitions. I just wanted to wrap my head around the whole concept. I never even saw a triathlon and didn't know the first thing about transitions.

We set up the bikes, and Coach Richie showed us the proper way to position our bike gear and running gear in front of the bike.

"Put the stuff that you need first in front," he said. "Make sure to put the helmet upside down on the seat and put your glasses in there, so you could easily pop it on and go."

Next, we ran with the bikes. After you dismount, you need to run a bit with the bike and Richie showed us how. The tri bikes seemed to handle the running a lot better than my road bike. I was running and the road bike was all over the place. I just couldn't get it straight.

Richie and one of my teammates told me to run faster, but running fast in cycling shoes is not the easiest thing to do . . . I tried anyway!

Things I learned at the clinic:

- Don't fuss with your hair. Either put it in a low pony or braids and keep it like that for the entire race, otherwise expect to lose time.
- Take your wetsuit off before you leave the water. Eric had a great point. He told me to take off the bathing cap and goggles then pull down the zipper on the wetsuit and take half of it off before you leave the water.
- Shed the socks. Richie told us it will be hard to put socks on wet feet so "wear your bike shoes and sneakers without socks," he said. I asked him what about blisters, and he said that there are some sneakers that don't give blisters, so you have to find an option that works.
- Wear a visor instead of a cap. My teammates agreed that a visor is quicker to put on than a cap.
- Get a running belt. I've been using the iFitness belt that I bought at the Disney Tower of Terror Expo the year before. It's comfortable and holds a lot, but it isn't light, especially when there is fluid in my two eight-ounce bottles. Coach Richie and the rest of the team told me to dump it. "You don't need hydration for a 5K," said one of the women on the team. "They have water on the course." Richie agreed and said I need a place to hang my number. "You can wear it around the back and then when you approach the finish line bring it to the front. This way, it won't bother you," he said.

- Get a tri bag—I went to the clinic with five bags filled with different gear. When Coach Richie saw what I had, he told me to go out and buy a tri bag that would hold everything for the triathlon including the wetsuit, sneakers, helmet, cycling gear, etc.

Richie showed the team some mounting and dismounting techniques but, for me, as a newbie, I thought I would just go with what I know, which is to stop the bike, put my leg over a tilted bike, put my foot on the pedal, and go.

At this point, if I tried any new techniques, I think I would fall and break something . . .

Lesson Learned

Be open to trying new things and taking advice from the experts. Trying something new is fun. When I learned to play golf a few years back, I just loved it and tried to learn everything I could about the sport. I felt the same with triathlons. There is so much to learn, so much to explore, and then there are the races. Everything is new, exciting, and invigorating. Go for it. Do something out of your wheelhouse, no matter what it is. And don't get down on yourself for not being able to get it right away. Give yourself a break and embrace change.

CHAPTER 13

First Two Triathlons

Up until this point, I had never seen an actual triathlon race. My coach insisted I watch him race in Riverhead, which was approximately ninety minutes east of my home. When I went out to see him at Riverhead Rocks, it was incredibly exciting. I watched as he swam, went into T1, biked, went into T2, and finished it up with the run. It helped me to put the whole race into perspective. Boy was he fast!

RACE 1: CAPTIVA TRI

At this point, I had been training for the Captiva Triathlon for nearly three months. The triathlon training was rough. Six days a week, I swam, biked, ran, or did a brick workout. It was especially tough since swimming and cycling were new to me. Although it was rough, it really prepared me for the race, and I don't think I would have been able to do the Captiva Tri without the coaching.

Becky and I flew down to Fort Myers on the Friday evening before the Sunday race. From the time we got on the plane until the day of the race, things got a little crazy. First, we had issues with our rental car company, then we got totally lost, all while being nervous wrecks!

The next day, we had a ton of things to do to prepare for the race. We both got up at 6:30 a.m. and planned a schedule for the day:

- 8:30 a.m.—Pick up the bikes at Billy's Bike Rental Shop in Sanibel (forty-five minutes away from where we stayed in Captiva)
- 10:30 a.m.—Swim clinic in the Gulf
- 12:00 p.m.—Transition workshop
- 1:00 p.m.—Lunch
- 2:00 p.m.—Twenty-minute bike ride and ten-minute run (like my coach wanted)
- 3:30 p.m.—Pick up race numbers and tattoos
- 5:00 p.m.—Meet up with Becky's family members.

The schedule was tight, so we were off. Billy's Bike Shop was a pleasure to work with. When we first started this journey, I thought I would have to ship the bikes and realized it was very expensive. The store manager got us two carbon fiber bikes to rent. He then fit us on the bikes. They cost us seventy-five dollars for the bikes and then an additional fifteen dollars for the pedals. The guys put the bikes in the back of the SUV, and we drove forty-five minutes back to the hotel just in time for the swim clinic.

The swim clinic was scary. The waves were rough, and the water was choppy. The athletes in the water were flapping and flailing their arms and legs in every direction. I was having issues as usual with my nose plugs. I had bought a bunch of the plastic kind. Later, I realized that the metal ones worked better. The plastic ones kept falling off, and when I tried to breathe without them, I couldn't swim. So, I stopped and put them on. I felt totally defeated after the clinic and didn't think I would be able to complete the race.

After that, Becky and I went on a bike ride, and I found that my bike was squeaking terribly. We had to put it back in the car and go back to the shop. That took another forty-five minutes each way . . .

It was 2:30 p.m. when we got back to our huge two-bedroom apartment on the beach at the South Seas Island Resort. We were exhausted, and I was in total panic mode.

Becky stayed calm throughout the day until we picked up our race numbers. She got the number 666. Then she lost it. She refused to put it on. The race director told her that if she didn't want to wear it, she couldn't race. This went on for nearly an hour in the hot sun until Becky said, "Why don't you wear the number 666 on your body?" That's when the race director got up and gave her a different number.

We got back to the hotel and decided to buy pasta and sauce from the company store. I texted Richie and he wrote me back, "Don't sweat the small stuff, it will be okay." We cooked up the pasta and then I crashed from being on high anxiety all day.

RACE DAY!

My alarm went off at 4 a.m. I jumped out of bed and put on my race gear. I braided my hair and was ready by 4:15 a.m. I started the coffee pot. Becky was still sleeping. I heard her alarm go off and she came out of the bedroom. "You're up already and ready to go?" she asked.

The night before, we talked about being at the transition area at 5:15 a.m. It closed at 6:45 a.m., but we wanted ample time to put our stuff out and get ready for the big day. This was our first triathlon, and we didn't know what to expect.

We left the house at 5 a.m. and rode our bicycles about a mile and a half in the dark to the race site. There were some cars that passed us, and they offered temporary lighting, but for the most part, we rode without lights. It was frightening.

When we got to the transition area, we walked in and found our spots. I was number #616 and Becky was #508, so we were in different sections. I racked the bike the way Richie showed me. Then, I proceeded to put down my transition mat. My bike shoes, helmet, and glasses went in front so that I could easily get them on before un-racking my bike. In the back, I put my race belt, sneakers, visor, and fluids. Everything was neatly organized.

There were a lot of first-timers there, so their stuff was all over the place. Some people spread out while others were compact. Some had their gear in the front of the bikes while others at the rear. I put mine compactly by the front wheel of the bike.

After I finished, I went to find Becky. I wanted to make one more pitstop to the bathroom and borrowed her flip flops. After using the Porta-Potty, I heard my number called. "Number #616 please report to your bike."

I dropped off Becky's flip flops and ran to my bike. "You're not in the right spot," said a volunteer. "You're in the wrong area."

I got a bit frantic. I ran around looking for the right spot. Found it. Pulled my bike off the rack and ran back to get all my gear. Becky found me and helped me set up.

After I was settled, Becky said, "Let's go to the water and warm up before the race."

Barefoot, we followed the crowd to the water. We stepped on shells and other hard objects along the way, which was brutal on our feet. When we got to the race start, which was about a quarter of a mile away, we put on our caps. I had a pink one and she had a white one because we were in different age groups. And we went into the water. I swam out to the buoy and back. I wanted to make sure I could do this. I did it without a hitch and felt confident, even though the last buoy looked far away. We both came out of the water and waited for our groups to be called.

The elite racers were off, followed by the white caps, Becky's group. There were a few more groups that went in the water before the pink caps went in. When the horn blew, everyone with the pink caps ran into the water. It was insane. Everyone was in a panic. I later learned that this happens all the time during the swim portion.

People were throwing their arms all over the place. People were kicking and punching me as I swam so that I wouldn't get in their space, and they would be the first ones out of the water. But I didn't let that bother me. I was kicking and punching people, too. There were a lot of people in the water, but I felt safe. There were plenty of lifeguards there, too.

As I swam, I kept thinking to myself, I could do this; the nose plugs won't fall off. I didn't stop. I kept moving my arms and kicking my legs. The first buoy came and went. I had one more to go. I could do this. I got this. I kept thinking about what Richie said, "Just swim your heart out." I also thought about Coach Bryan, saying, "Just swim and take it easy and breathe. Don't panic."

I tried to stay calm and relaxed. I finally got to the last buoy and turned toward the beach. I swam until I felt the bottom and then stood up and ran out of the water. There were a ton of people cheering us on. I tried to stay focused and get to T1 as soon as possible.

I ran into the transition area, found my bike and gear. I dried off my feet and put on my bicycle shoes, my helmet, glasses, and picked up the bike from the rack and ran out of transition. I got to the mount line, got on my bike, and rode five miles down a winding road. There were some sharp turns on the road and, when we got to mile five, there was a sharp U-turn. There were a ton of men passing me screaming, "On your left." Some of them came so close to me, I thought my bike would fall over. I felt as if I were in the Tour de France, or maybe they thought they were!

I was trying to go as fast as I could. I really couldn't gauge how fast I was going because there was no cadence sensor on the bike. So, I just tried to follow people. I kept spotting the same man with a white t-shirt. I passed him, he passed me, and we kept going back and forth. When I was behind him, I tried to keep up with his cadence and go faster.

The roads were bumpy and rough. My bottom wasn't happy, but I kept going. I didn't even want to grab a drink for the fear of slowing down!

I approached the dismount line and unclipped my pedals. The man in front of me dismounted early and, since he was directly in front, I had to dismount too. I ran the bike back into the transition area for T2.

I quickly found my spot, took off my gear, put on my sneakers and racing belt, and I was off. There were tons of people walking out of T2 to the run, which slowed me down. I wanted to be able to run the three miles but found that between my breathing and a hamstring strain, I had to walk a little. I had injured my hamstring during training, but I pushed through.

I wasn't alone. There were plenty of walkers.

Injuries are a part of life for any athlete. They totally suck but when you get them, you just have to either grin and bear it until it heals, or you need to rest. Rest is often preferred.

We ran around the golf course twice. It had different terrain than I was used to—gravel, stone, and sand. It went up and it went down. There was no shade, and, at that point, it was getting very hot. During my first lap out, I heard, "Hey, Hilary . . ." I looked over and there was Becky about 100 feet ahead of me. I don't know how she saw me, but she did, and I wasn't sure if she was on her first or second lap.

On the path, I met a young woman who reminded me of my daughter. She was walking. I was running behind her and passed her and said, "We can do this . . ."

After mile one, I kept trying to focus on my kids and how much they mean to me. They both were so supportive during this training process, and the fact that they believed in me and believed that I could do this got me through mile two. I walked a little after mile two and found a man named Troy. He was thirty-five and was also walking. I knew his age because everyone's age is stamped on the back of their calves. Not sure why they do this in a triathlon, but apparently, it's common practice. I encouraged him to run when I felt my breathing got more in control. We started to talk a little.

We both got each other through the end of the race and through the finish line where I threw up my arms and screamed, "I did it!"

It was one of the most emotional races I have ever competed in. Here I was in my fifties doing something so out of my comfort zone. And I did it. I completed it. I felt so good and so proud of myself. I started to cry.

When I crossed the finish line, I was given a medal and a cold towel. I looked for Becky, but I didn't see her. I knew she was ahead of me, so I headed over to the transition area and thought she could still be there.

I didn't see her and decided to wait. I called my coach and told him about the experience.

"Did you call your family yet?" he asked.

"No, you were the first one I called because you're my coach," I said. "And anyway, everyone in my house is probably sleeping!"

He congratulated me and told me he was proud of my accomplishment, which really meant a lot to me because he was the type of coach that if you miss a workout, he was not happy and let you know it!

I finally found Becky. We went over to see how we did and found out that we were only three minutes apart.

My Time:
- Swim: 00:12:37
- T1: 00:03:25
- Cycle: 00:39:02
- T2: 00:02:06
- Run: 00:40:22
- **Total time: 1:37:30**

We hugged and expressed that it was amazing to complete our first triathlon together!

Since I loved this race so much, I signed up for the Montauk triathlon, which was two weeks later.

RACE 2: MONTAUK RACE

About a month before Montauk, I read on Facebook that my friend, Jim Reed, was going to lose a leg. I didn't know what happened. I saw him more than a year before at the Long Beach Diner. He seemed fine. But sometimes looks can be deceiving.

Jim always commented on my Facebook posts, and one time, he asked if we could meet up. He told me he worked for the Department of Consumer Affairs. (Hmm . . . did I do something wrong?) We met a few times after that. Jim had a big heart and I enjoyed spending time with him.

I went to see him at the Grandell Rehabilitation and Nursing Center in Long Beach. Jim had a positive attitude, but I knew inside he was hurting. I felt I wanted to do more for him than just pick up a brisket sandwich from Lido Kosher Deli. I wanted to do something challenging that would honor his courage and inspiration. Since I had just signed up for the Montauk Sprint, I thought completing it would be a great way to honor him.

I knew the Montauk Sprint would be hard. It consisted of a half-mile swim, fourteen-mile bike, and a 5K run. I knew it would be harder for me, just getting over the hamstring injury and doing my first triathlon two weeks earlier. But that made it more of a challenge.

As the Montauk race became a reality, I had a lot of challenges—issues at work, disappointments with family members not being able to attend the race, and just daily life stresses, which provoked race anxiety.

Race morning, I woke up at 4 a.m., got dressed, and headed out the door to the race site. Becky came to my rescue by staying overnight at my hotel that I booked across from the race site, and she helped calm me before the race.

When I arrived at the site, I saw my teammates from the All Women's Tri Team (AWTT), this was another team I joined. I loved the team because it was made up of a diverse group of women. Many tri groups you can only get into if you hire a coach who leads the group. So, if you are coached, you're in. But others, like the AWTT, you can join and feel a part of the family. I also saw my teammates from Tri-Global. I appreciated their love and support at that moment because I really needed it.

As I was putting out my gear on my transition mat, I started to run the race through my head. My coach saw me contemplating. "What are you doing?" he asked. I told him and he told me to stop. "You know what to do, just go out there and do it," he said.

After being marked up with my number, 266, and my age, which was fifty-two at the time, I put on my wetsuit and white bathing cap and followed a stream of people to Fort Pond. The white caps were last before the relay racers. We waited. I stood with a teammate from AWTT.

When it was our turn into the water, we went in halfway. The countdown began—three, two, one, and then the horn blew, and we were on our way out approximately 375 meters and back for a total of 750 meters.

I started to swim and immediately got kicked in the ribs by the woman in front of me. I stopped and started choking. She knocked the wind out of me.

"Are you okay?" she asked, looked at me as I nodded, and she swam away.

I took several strokes with my head out of the water. I started hyperventilating. I kept stopping along the way out. I couldn't catch my breath. People were swimming by me. I felt as if I already lost the race. I didn't see anyone behind me, and I started to panic. I felt as if the sky started to cave down on me and I would never be able to get out of the water.

A woman on the paddle board stopped me and said, "Just relax for a few minutes. Don't do anything until your breathing is back to normal. Then take ten strokes and you'll be fine."

I loved the fact that the water was fresh water and not salty. I looked over at the sun and saw it rising. I thought about Jim and thought I could do this for him. I must do this for Jim.

So, I took ten strokes and felt okay. Then, I took twenty and twenty became forty, and before I knew it, I was at land. I did it. I felt like I lost so much time from being kicked, and I wasn't feeling mentally good about the race at that point. But I carried on.

Once out of the water, I tried to remember what to take off first—the bathing cap and goggles or the wetsuit? I remembered Eric saying, "Take off the wetsuit while you're still in the water." The wetsuit came off halfway first, and then I started removing everything else.

My transition in T1 was faster than the one in Florida without a wetsuit. I knew I needed to make up time.

I got on the bike and rode away. I passed a woman on the left. She was taking her time. I didn't understand why. After that, I saw very few people on their bikes. I wanted to tag behind someone to gauge how fast I was going but there really wasn't anyone there. I rode as fast as I could, up and down the hills of Montauk. This was something I feared prior to the race, and when I told my coach that I was afraid of the hills, he said, "They are just freaking hills." So, I focused on that.

The ride was magnificent. I was a little nervous with the cars on the road, but everyone seemed aware that we were there. Riding up the hills burned my thighs and riding down them made me incredibly nervous. I wanted to brake, but I held myself back. I knew this was my only opportunity to make up time. I went twenty-six miles an hour on the downhill according to my Garmin 910xt! It felt fast.

The miles seemed to pass by quickly, and this time, I made sure to drink water. In Captiva, I didn't want to attempt to drink because I feared I would drop my water bottle in the road. This time, I didn't care.

I saw the dismount, slowed down, and unclipped my shoes. I got off the bike and ran into T2. I changed quickly and was out on the run within a minute or so. As I started, I saw Coach Richie. He ended up running with me for three miles. This time, I didn't stop. He wouldn't let me. The only break I got was on the water stop, where I had a few sips of water and kept on running. I started feeling knee twinges and back pain, but I ran through it.

The run was beautiful. It circled around Fort Pond. My coach was amazing on the run too. He was motivating and encouraging. I needed that. I kept thinking about the bad swim and how I could have done better. He told me to let it go. It was hard for me to do that. About 2.5 miles in, Coach Richie told me I was on my own and to pick up the pace.

The race wasn't easy. But as I started approaching the finish line, I got a bit of energy and ran as fast as I could to cross the finish line. I ran this 5K in thirty-five minutes. This was my fastest 5K ever!

As I crossed the finish line, I said out loud, "I did it for you, Jim . . . You're going to pull through this . . ."

I didn't finish last. There were others who followed me.

I saw Becky, who handed me my tri bag, and I went back to the transition area to pack up. I was disappointed. I felt as if I didn't do as well as Captiva, even though this was a much harder race. As I was packing up, my phone rang . . .

"Hilary, you won your division," Coach Richie said on the line.

"How could that be? I felt like I screwed up the whole thing."

"You need to come over here right now to get your award," he said.

I was in shock. I went over to the award area, and they called my name. I was handed a plaque, a dozen yummy, delicious cookies that were baked at a local bakery, and a twenty-dollar gift card to Brands Cycle and Fitness shop in Wantagh. After I collected my award, Constance told me to go to the podium. I went up there for a photo. I was proud of my accomplishments but was still shocked that I won first place in my division.

I went to visit Jim and presented him with my medal. I thought it was more appropriate for him to have it than for me to have it. A couple of months later, sadly, Jim passed away.

Lesson Learned

Find something inspiring to help keep you going, like I did in this race for Jim. Don't get yourself wrapped up in what you did or a poor performance—all that matters is how you finished. Sometimes, when you think you did badly, there might be others who may have done worse. Or, you could be the only one in your age group. Whatever the case, don't leave at the end of a triathlon. Find out your results. Hey, you never know, you could have placed!

2015

"I tell myself everything in life is impermanent. If I'm suffering, I remind myself the pain will pass and bring my mind back to a positive thought and visualize myself finishing whatever leg I am doing one step at a time. I tell myself repeatedly—you can do it, you are strong, you are capable."

–Katelyn J. Hughes, Ironman, New York

CHAPTER 14

Working With a New Coach

FEBRUARY

After Montauk, I started to re-evaluate my season and decided to interview another coach. I liked Richie, but I thought it was time for a change.

I interviewed a handful of local coaches and decided to hire Danielle Sullivan of Iron Fit Endurance. Danielle was a pro-triathlete and she really impressed me. I felt I clicked with her, and I had a gut feeling that she could get me to the next level. She was easy to talk with and had a positive attitude.

I sat down with Danielle those first few weeks and we mapped out a plan. Honestly, I think I made her crazy because I wanted to do so many races that year. I was so hooked on the sport and wanted to experience as many races as I could that "true first year." But she was patient with me and, most importantly, she was flexible.

Danielle encouraged me to join a different master swim program that was closer to my home because she thought I would benefit from it. But, getting up at 5 a.m. was difficult, especially when I had tossed and turned all night long!

However, the master's swim class was held on Wednesdays at 6:30 a.m. and ran until 7:45 a.m. and, since I knew the coach, Maggie, I decided to go.

Maggie was a tall, muscular blonde from Slovakia. She was an Olympian and an amazing swimmer and coach. I loved her smile, her enthusiasm, and she kept the group laughing every time we took a rest during the set.

The first time I met Maggie she looked at my bathing suit and laughed.

"What are you wearing? That bathing suit is way too big!"

I couldn't believe it. I always bought larger-sized bathing suits because I felt so self-conscious. She told me it was at least three sizes too big!

"It will create drag in the water," she told me.

I went home after the swim and purchased a few size 4 bathing suits on SwimOutlet.com. I could barely get into them. I remember the first time I wore a size four, everything was hanging out. I went to see Maggie and she said, "Now that's the right size!" I laughed and shook my head.

I got used to it and I felt less self-conscious. I also got used to wearing goggles, ear plugs, and nose plugs. I never realized how much the water impacted your ears and sinuses!

Maggie was an incredible swim coach and helped me get from just learning how to swim to learning how to swim efficiently. At that point, I was averaging around three minutes for 100 yards.

What I loved about Maggie's coaching was that she would tell you what you were doing right and what you were doing wrong, and she taught you how to correct it. She knew everyone's time and knew how to push to get you to the next level.

On one of my swim training days, I jumped in the pool a little late and didn't get a chance to warm up, so I used the drill section to warm up. There were six people in my lane, which was fifty meters in length.

Bill led the lane, followed by Paul and Joan. I followed and quickly moved up to swim behind Paul. The problem with the group was that we all swam around the same pace, so there were times where we were all on top of each other. I decided after that happened several times, to take fifteen seconds in between so that Joan, or Bill, or Paul, or whoever, had plenty of time to take off.

The drills were eight 50s consisting of kicks, backstroke, speed stroke, and relaxed freestyle. Then the main set.

"We're going to swim for a mile broken up today," said Maggie. "I want you to do two 250s, five 100s, and ten 50s . . ."

"What?" I don't know why I couldn't comprehend . . . maybe it was not enough sleep, maybe it was too early in the morning.

She said it again and again and again . . . Okay, now it stuck.

We took off. The first 250, I wore my fins. I went last and quickly caught up and passed each member of the group. Bill, the fastest swimmer who also was a collegiate swimmer, gave me such a strange look in the water as I passed him. When I was finished, I was so way ahead of everyone, and Maggie said, "Ok, now take off your fins."

"Why?" I asked

"Because you're the only one wearing them," she said. I took them off. I still had a long way to go and was forcing myself to move forward.

After the second 250, three of the swimmers left to get ready for work. Paul, Bill, and I stayed and still had plenty to go.

When we finished our five 100s, we started to do ten 50's. At the "rest stop," I said, "How many more?" And Maggie said, "Eight more!"

"Jesus . . ." I said.

"Do you think Jesus will help?" she said.

"I can pray and hope so," I said and smiled.

I finished swimming 2,460 yards and felt completely and utterly pooped!

Mental Health

It's hard to not let triathlons define you. You work hard. You train. You do what you need to do, and sometimes even beyond that. And, although the competition is within yourself, it's hard not to compare yourself with other people's accomplishments. Doing so can make you feel bad and question why you are doing this.

For me, it was always easy to drift into feeling down about myself and getting depressed. Having no emotional or financial support my entire life, I always felt like I had to fight for everything I wanted. Reflecting, I wonder if no support or encouragement made me a stronger person. Maybe?

RUNNING IN THE HEAT

Danielle encouraged me to run in different conditions to get used to it. She put eight miles on the Training Peaks schedule, so I decided to do it on the path by the Wantagh Parkway. I figured four miles out from Wantagh to Jones Beach and four miles back. It seemed doable. I've done it dozens of times this year without a problem. But on this day, it was a problem.

The first mile, my knee started bothering me, but I ignored it. The second mile was okay. Mile three and four started getting rough, but I forced myself not to turn around. I only had two eight-ounce bottles of water and a couple of packets of gel. I was finding myself reaching for the water more often than I thought I would. There was no water or shade on that route.

It was hot. The air was still, and I was having a hard time breathing. I felt as if there was no oxygen. I started to see black spots during mile four and by mile five I was walking. I tried to find shade. I just needed to sit and get my heart rate down. It was at 145 bpm while walking. I was running out of water. I saw an older couple taking a break and I asked them if I could get some water from them. The man was kind enough to fill up my eight-ounce bottle. I drank it. It tasted great. I needed that. Miles five, six, and seven were torture. I walked most of the way. I tried to run, but I couldn't get enough air, and it was so dry and so hot I just felt as if I couldn't go on. I looked down at my legs and arms and noticed that I had a heat rash. The inside of my legs was burning from the scraping of my shorts.

When will this be over? I kept asking myself. Another 1.5 miles to go.

I called my husband. "I can't go on," I said. "I don't think I'm going to make it. I'm dizzy. I see black spots and I'm getting a rash all over my body."

He told me to take it easy and take my time. I was hoping he would say, "Oh don't worry honey, I'll come get you." But he didn't.

Finally, I saw the mile sign to Cedar Park. Okay, I thought, I could do this. Just a little more to go. I kept wishing there was water. I was sweating so much everything was sticking to me. I started to feel depressed that I wasn't accomplishing this workout. I wanted to do those eight miles in one hour and twenty minutes, and instead, it was taking me more than two hours. I was feeling frustrated. I couldn't give up because if I did, I would feel even worse.

When I finally reached my car, I turned on the air conditioning and drank a twenty-four-ounce bottle of water that I had sitting on ice.

RIDING AERO FOR THE FIRST TIME

Ever since I bought my Trek Silque road bike in June, I had been uncomfortable. So, I decided to buy aero bars—handlebar extensions that attach to the center of the handlebar.

I went to a bike store in Wantagh, and the bike fitter helped select an aero bar he thought would be right for me. He asked one of the bike mechanics to put them on. Now, my bike looked totally different.

Around the time that I purchased my bike, I also purchased an indoor trainer. This enabled me to make my bike a stationary bike. After, I put the aero bars on the bike, I went home and tried them out on my indoor trainer. It felt comfortable.

But it wasn't until I went out with Coach Danielle for a ride with them that I got the feel of going aero. Now, for those of you who have never ridden in an aero position, I can attest, it is very different than what you are used to.

First off, you're in a very different position. You're leaning all the way over and riding. It's very scary at first. You feel like you have no control of the road, until you get the hang of it.

These are the rules I learned when going aero:

1. Never turn in aero.
2. To get into aero position, bring the stronger hand over to the bar first then the weaker hand. Danielle told me she uses her right hand first. But since I use my right to keep the bike steady, I preferred to use my left arm first.
3. Switch from regular position to aero on a slow flat smooth road. Try switching off for a few miles to get used to it.
4. Don't stay in aero on hills just straightaways.

I was grateful I tried this out with Danielle by my side because I think I would have been unsuccessful doing it on my own. I felt shaky at first and was a little nervous about falling, but within the hour we spent together, I was able to get it!

Lesson Learned

There were a few lessons learned here.

For starters, that eight-mile run–walk wasn't pretty, but I dug deep and finished it . . . I started to think that nothing in my life came easy. I wanted to go to college, but my parents discouraged it. So, I worked full-time to put myself through school. I wanted to start a business but had no money, so I found a way to make it happen. There were always obstacles along the way, but you can never give up. If you do, everyone who discourages you wins.

As for hydrating, when you run long distances, it's important to have electrolytes in your water along with some nutrition to help get you through the workout. Drink an ounce or two at least once every fifteen minutes or so, then take a gel every thirty to forty minutes.

And finally, when you're learning a new sport, have patience with yourself. Don't get aggravated that you're not catching on, it will come. Keep at it, and you will ace whatever sport you put your mind to!

CHAPTER 15

Triathlon Training Camp

When I first started to play golf, I went to golf camp up in Mount Snow and had an amazing experience. So, when the opportunity came up to go to triathlon camp with the AWTT, I was thrilled.

Open Sky Training was owned by Coach Ed Gabriels. He and his wife owned a beautiful home in Germantown, New York. It had several bedrooms that were nicely decorated, a large living room, and den. Since Ed was a food stylist for a living, he prepared the meals and made them taste and look amazing!

Becky and I left Long Island at 4 p.m. and arrived at the camp at around 7 p.m. As soon as we walked in, we were greeted by teammates. Ed was there and told us that I was rooming with Diahann, and Becky would be rooming with Jamie. John, another coach there who was also a triathlete and English Channel swimmer, told us to put on our running gear and that we were going for a run.

After a series of active warm-ups, we ran for about three miles and then headed back to the house for a dinner of pasta and meat sauce. It was delicious!

The next day started early. We went for a two-hour-plus bike ride, through rolling hills and a few steep hills. John taught us how to ride the hills and how to shift, when to shift, and more! He was incredibly patient and understanding. After the ride, we went into the backyard and practiced mounting on the bike. After several of us fell, we started to get the hang of it . . . I know I needed a lot more practice!

We had a quick snack of some yummy peanut butter and bananas on a wrap, got into our bathing suits, and went for a swim at the pool at Bard College. John videotaped us and gave us individualized attention to make our swim stronger. He also taught us how to sight in open water, how to swim straight by closing our eyes while we were swimming, and he critiqued our strokes. It was helpful.

We went back to the house, had lunch, and rested for two hours. Diahann and I just passed out on our beds. I'm sure everyone else did as well. After our nap, we gathered our wetsuits and went to the lake for an open water swim.

The water was cold, but not that cold. We all went in. John told us just to hang out and relax in the water before we got started. Ed joined us. I was a little nervous that I would have a panic attack. At first, I found it difficult to put my face in the water because it was so cold.

John told us to take twenty strokes and stop. He gave us a point to focus on for our sighting. I started to coach myself: I don't have problems in the pool, I shouldn't have problems here . . . I got this. We swam some more. Now we were in the middle of the lake. Some of my teammates were having panic attacks and I stayed with them. "You got this," I told them. By helping them, it took the focus off me, and I was able to do it without any problems.

John split us into two groups. One group headed back, and the other group went in a triangle around the lake. I went with the latter group. At first, I fell behind. Then, my wetsuit opened. I could feel a cold stream of water go around my body. It felt good. I asked a teammate to help. She stopped, zipped me up, and we were on our way to the rest of the group.

When we finally made it back to the shoreline, I told John and Ed that I had to take the wetsuit off. I find it so restricting. I wanted to swim in the water without it. And, boy, I had absolutely no problem. I felt free.

I could swim like that forever! I headed over to a floating dock in the middle of the lake. Ed followed me and so did John. Ed climbed up and sat down. I followed him and John followed me.

"You know I've never been on this dock before," Ed told me.

Ed and John were joking around, and I felt as if I were fifteen again with my high school friends, just being silly. We jumped off the dock, well, they jumped, I edged my way in, and we swam to shore to meet up with the rest of the team.

The next day, Becky, Diahann, and I went to the pool at Bard College. That was when all the fun began. Just as I thought I knew how to swim, John changed everything—the stroke, the way we breathe, and the positioning of our bodies. I was so confused but understood that he was spot on with this and that if I could master it, I would go faster.

The tri camp ended with a delicious BBQ, a little wine, and hugs from everyone. Not only did I learn something from the weekend, but I also bonded with the most incredible group of women.

Lesson Learned

If you can go away for training camp, do it. The benefits outweigh the time and cost. Going to triathlon training camp, or any other "sport" camp, will help you become more equipped to handle the sport, both physically and mentally. It will also enable you to meet like-minded people who are also in your sport. The amazing people you meet will become your lifelong friends.

CHAPTER 16

My 2015 Race Season—Hang on to Your Seat!

My first race of the season was in March—Las Olas Sprint Triathlon in Fort Lauderdale. I arrived in Fort Lauderdale on Wednesday to help my dad. While down there from New York, I decided to sign up for a triathlon. I knew I needed to come in March and the timing worked out perfect for the Las Olas Triathlon. I also wanted my dad to experience what I love to do.

Check in on Saturday was a breeze. I rented a Specialized Ruby bike from Bike America in Coral Springs. It was smooth to ride.

I brought everything else with me, my TYR Hurricane wetsuit, my bike shoes, and my Zoot running shoes.

I was staying at my dad's house in Tamarac. He had a lovely two-bedroom apartment in Kings Point that he and my mom bought a few years after they moved to Florida.

The next day, I arrived at 6 a.m. on the dot at the race site. I dragged my dad with me. Transition had opened at 6:00, and people were already checked in. There was a huge line to get into transition.

"Body markings only," the woman screamed in my ear. I found out where body markings were taking place, and it was such a long line.

Body markings are imperative at a triathlon. Each athlete gets a number that is unique to them, and you need to wear it throughout the race. Sometimes, the race organizers will give you a temporary tattoo, or a volunteer will mark you with an indelible marker.

I told my dad to take a seat as it would be a while. The line was over a block long! I was a little worried about him because he often got lost, but I figured he would stay put. This was the first race he ever attended and my third triathlon race.

The line went faster than I had thought it would and within minutes, I was being marked with number 783 and given a chip around my leg. Then, I set up transition. The whole process was making me very anxious.

When I got to transition, I was next to a man who told me to place my stuff by my front wheel. He was adamant about it, and I just went with the flow.

The announcer told everyone to leave transition by 7 a.m. I only had fifteen minutes to set up and put on my wetsuit, which, as you know, usually takes me a long time. I started to panic.

"Okay everyone must leave the transition area now," the announcer said.

I left. I brought a bottle of electrolyte water with me. I forgot the gel.

As I left transition, I saw my dad. He found a bridge chair from one of the unattended booths and was sitting on it by the beach. I felt a little embarrassed because he took one of the volunteers' chairs, but that was my dad. So, I brushed it off.

The sun was starting to rise. The sky was breathtaking. I knew it would be a great day. As I was talking with my dad, I looked over my shoulder and saw a woman. She looked familiar. She looked at me.

"Hilary?" she said.

"OMG, DEBBIE I CAN'T BELIEVE I'M SEEING YOU!" I screamed. I was so excited. I hadn't seen my friends Debbie and Eric for nearly seven years. They had always been very close personal friends. My husband and I went to college with them.

"What are you doing here?"

"What are you doing here?" she asked me. They had relocated to Florida several years ago. "I'm here because Ryan is a triathlete, and this is his first race." I hadn't seen their son, Ryan, since he was a little boy.

"Wow, that is so cool!" I couldn't believe how much he changed! "I'm here because I came down to help my dad with a few things and I signed up for this," I told her.

The three of us picked up from where we left off years ago, as if time never stopped.

When I turned around again, I saw my brother, Ed and sister-in-law, Andrea. "I'm so glad to see you," I told them. They lived in South Florida, too. Then I saw their three sons, Max, Ben, and Jacob. I was incredibly excited to see so many familiar faces, especially family members who I dearly missed. This was the first race that I had family attend and it made me so happy to share this huge part of my life with them.

It was now 8 a.m. An hour went by since I left transition and I wanted to go down by the water and wait for my wave. My wave was supposed to go off at 8:23 a.m.

I started to talk with other women with a "pink" cap. I asked them if they knew what was going on. No one knew. There seemed to be no organization.

At 8:30 a.m., the organizers started to set up by where we were all standing. They were originally located a half a mile away for the international triathlon but had to break everything down and come to where the sprint people were hanging out.

Everyone was complaining. But they set up quickly, and by 8:40 a.m., we were on our way.

I met a woman from the Boca Raton Triathletes, and we talked for a while. She told me she used to live in Rockville Centre, which was close to my home.

"I typically come in last at these things," she said. I nodded my head. "So do I." Once we were in the water, I lost her and didn't see her again until the end.

The swim was deadly for me. I started to panic. I felt as if I couldn't get into a rhythm and found it hard to swim. I felt like I just started swimming, which was only nine months before. I forgot how to breathe. I was hyperventilating. I had to hold on to the safety kayaks in the water at least two times. I started to feel frustrated. Will I ever get out of the water?

I kept thinking, I'm almost there, I can do this and, before I knew it, I was out of the water. I was one of the last ones, but I was out.

I could barely run to transition. I was out of breath and totally exhausted. I walked in calmly, put on my shoes, like my coach told me to, put on my helmet, and was out with the bike.

I ran the bike out of T1 and mounted at the mounting line. I found the bike to be incredibly easy to ride and very comfortable.

I got on easily and took off. I tried to go out hard. It was an incredibly smooth ride. I loved every minute of it. I rode through the streets of downtown Fort Lauderdale and through a park. When I was at the park there were no arrows, and I wasn't sure if I was going in the right direction. That's when I slowed down significantly. I didn't see anyone for a long time until someone passed me on the left. That's when I knew I was on the right path.

I left the park and tried to make up some time. Meanwhile, there were two steep bridges that we went over. I was not anticipating that. But I was easily able to make it up the hill. The ride down was incredible. I just coasted and braked when I got to a sharp turn in the road.

The bike path was gorgeous. We rode along the water and then through a lush park and back along the beach.

I was told to slow it down as I approached dismount and slowly braked and unclipped. I ran into transition, racked the bike, put the helmet down, put on my running shoes, and I was on my way out of transition.

The run was also beautiful, along A1A with a breathtaking view of the beach and the Atlantic Ocean. The water was turquoise blue. The only thing that made the run hard was the heat. It was in the nineties and very humid.

I found it hard to run and felt dehydrated. I ate a gel and that helped a little, but I was still very dry. At every water stop, I poured water on my head and drank as much as I could without choking from rushing.

Early in the run, I met up with a woman from the Boca Triathlon Team. She was doing the Run Walk Run method—thirty seconds running, thirty seconds walking. I decided to join her. My breathing was so heavy even though I took a spritz of asthma medicine.

The method worked and we still ran at a decent pace. When we saw the finish line, we sprinted. It certainly made the run go faster and we got to know each other a little better.

As I crossed the finish line, my sister-in-law was standing there. "I'm so proud of you!" she said. We hugged.

I saw my old friends, Debbie and Eric, and found out that Ryan placed second in his age group! Not too shabby for his first tri!

I also saw my brother and my nephews. They were so excited to see me finish. I was so excited to see them.

But most importantly, I saw my dad, who kissed me and said, "I am proud of you." This was the first time he ever said this to me in my life. He absolutely loved watching the race, and having him there to witness this meant everything to me. It motivated me and kept me inspired to keep coming down to Florida to do more races.

On this trip to Tamarac, I spent the rest of the weekend with my dad and his girlfriend. His girlfriend insisted that my dad spend time with me. He seemed lost without her, but we were able to talk, and he mentioned that he was so sorry that he "beat me as a child."

"I really feel bad about it," he said. I told him I forgave him and to let it go.

Lesson Learned

Bring a family member or close friend with you to a triathlon or other athletic event. It means so much to have someone there and when you finish it becomes more meaningful.

CHAPTER 17

Going Overboard With Races

After Las Olas, I did the Power of a Woman Pool Triathlon in Eisenhower Park on Long Island. The pool swim was a 400-meter swim, a six-mile bike, and a two-mile run. It was a blast, but I found myself competing with Becky and it started to make me feel uncomfortable. I didn't want to compete with her. I wanted us to be as we were while we raced in the "old days." But I realized in my heart during that race, that since we went with different coaches, things would never be the same.

Following that, I went out to the East End, on the North Fork of Long Island and did a race called the Mighty North Fork Race, which I thought was going to be easy.

I heard the swim was like a lake, and the bike and run were flat and fast. But I didn't find that to be the case. It was tough, but I talked my way through it. As I got to the finish line, a guy from the Wildwood Warriors, a triathlon team on Long Island, said in his loudspeaker, "Go Iron Fit Endurance! Danielle Sullivan would be so proud!" He made me laugh.

JULY AND THE NYC TRIATHLON—JUMPING IN THE HUDSON RIVER!

The last couple of weeks leading up to the New York City Triathlon were intense. I couldn't sleep, and all I kept thinking about was the fear of jumping in the Hudson River, finding something that didn't belong in a river like a dead body, and climbing up steep hills on the Henry Hudson Parkway. I started to have a defeatist attitude. I can't do this! Why did I bother signing up? This is out of my league!

The week before the race, I was on the phone with Danielle a lot. I couldn't focus on anything other than the race and thought seriously about getting a deferment or just not showing up.

I was still on the fence up until Friday before the race. That morning, I had breakfast with a client and good friend, Joan, who put things in perspective.

Joan, who was a marketing director at a company I represented, asked, "What are you afraid of?"

"Jumping in the Hudson and climbing up some steep hills," I said.

"Hilary, you do this all the time and you're good at it . . ." she said, not referring to any race but referring to life and business. "Tell me how many times you jumped in or climbed hills," she said. I took this to heart, and I let it resonate. I started to focus on what she said.

She's right. I climb hills every day and I jump in dirty water. I need not fear this race, I told myself. I did this in business, and I could do this in triathlons.

The night before the race, we stayed at a hotel in Manhattan. A luxury bus picked us up at the hotel at 3:45 a.m. and took us to transition.

After setting up, we had to walk more than a mile to swim start. We waited and watched as the elite men took off in the Hudson River. While waiting, we saw used condoms and dead fish floating in the Hudson River. This made us even more nervous to jump in!

"OMG," I said to Becky. "Are we really going to do this?" She didn't answer and we kept moving forward.

When we went up to the swim start, Becky and I sat next to each other on the dock and jumped in the Hudson together. The river had a current, so we swam faster than we normally did. Unfortunately, the current has nothing to do with the way I sighted. Instead of looking straight toward the dock, I was off course and ended up swimming toward New Jersey.

When I turned in toward the sea wall, I accidentally bumped into a woman who pushed me and said, "Would you stop bumping into me?" I apologized but it wasn't my fault. I couldn't see a thing!

Once I got to the dock, there were three people pulling me up. I was tired from swimming the distance. I got on the dock and ran barefoot to transition, which was nearly three-quarters of a mile away.

Swim Time: 00:23:46

I changed out of my wetsuit, put on my bike helmet and bike shoes, and took my bike out of transition. I kept telling myself, "You can do this, you can make it up the hill. You made it up the hill in business when no one else believed in you. You can do it here."

When I got to the hill, it was okay. I climbed it. I didn't have to get off my bike. As a matter of fact, I never got off my bike during the entire twenty-six miles. I was so nervous that I wouldn't make the cutoff. I just kept going. I started not to care about my fear on the downhills or how hard it was on the uphill for me. I needed to be able to finish. I needed to prove to myself that I could do this. This couch potato could get this done.

Along the Henry Hudson Parkway, I saw lots of flat tires, dropped chains, and water bottles galore on the road, along with some hefty potholes. It was motivating to see my AWTT friends on the course screaming my name!

When the bike was finished, I was happy. I did two of the three disciplines.

Bike Time: 1:50:00

Now all I must do is run through Central Park. The only problem, it was more than ninety degrees and humid that day!

I put on my shoes and my cap and started to walk out of transition. I felt a twinge in my knee and a twinge in my back. I saw two of my teammates there, Lisa and Shidah, who ran out with me. I was grateful to Shidah for giving me some salt that I desperately needed. They took off. I continued to walk it off.

As we headed from Riverside Park to Central Park, there was a whole group from the AWTT cheering squad, headed up by Gail, who got the entire block to chant my name. Yes, I was a little embarrassed, but it was wonderful to get their support!

When I got into the park, I saw so many of my tri/running friends. It was awesome!

Every mile, I would stop at the medical tent and get a packet of salt, which I put on my tongue and chased it with water. I did this because I was rapidly losing electrolytes. I was sweating a lot and felt somewhat dizzy from the heat.

I also dumped a cup of cold water on my head to bring down the temperature in my body. The temperature outside was a humid ninety-five degrees and climbing!

At mile four, I saw Lisa from my office and her husband screaming out my name. It was so incredible to see them. I didn't think they would make it in since they lived upstate.

I became emotional when I saw Zoey, catching up to me at the water stop at mile five and walking beside me. "You've got this, Mom," she said, "The hard part is over. Just a mile left."

I shed a tear. It made me feel so good for her to come out and support me. I know my son would have come out too, but he was on vacation with my father in Hawaii. At that point, my father was in the early stages of Alzheimer's, and I told my son to always keep an eye on him. My son had just graduated from high school and my dad wanted to go on a trip with him. It made me feel good since my dad and I never got to go away together as he promised me when I was little.

I dug very deep to cross that finish line. Once I got there, I was extremely emotional. I called my coach and talked it over with her, and she was so excited for me. That made me feel amazing. I thought I couldn't do it. I was emotionally distraught about the race, but after talking with Joan, I was able to get through it with plenty of time to spare!

Run Time: 1:30:00

When I finished the New York City Triathlon, I went to my social media. My daughter wrote this on her post on Facebook:

"So proud of my mom for finishing the NYC triathlon! She is the strongest person I know and will always push herself, despite all obstacles, to achieve her goals. She inspires me every day. ♡*"*

SEPTEMBER AND THE NATIONAL CHAMPIONSHIP

When I received a letter inviting me to attend the USA Triathlon National Championship in Milwaukee, I thought it was a joke. Really? Why would I be invited? I'm new to the sport and not fast. But I realized I got in because I won my age group at the race in Montauk.

Thinking this was a once in a lifetime opportunity, I booked my trip and went solo to the event in Milwaukee.

Before I got on the plane, I called my coach. I had just completed the New York City Triathlon and my time was around four hours. I was reviewing the stats and found that most of the women in my age group completed the Olympic distance race (one-mile swim, 40K bike, and 10K run) in under three hours and thirty minutes. I was scared. The NYC Triathlon took me four hours and ten minutes.

"Maybe I shouldn't go," I told her.

"That's up to you, but it will be a great experience," she told me.

After pondering the decision of whether to go, I posted a status update on the AWTT's Facebook group page. Most of the folks told me to go for it. "If you come in last, you still competed against the best," many wrote.

I didn't realize what I was getting myself into. I arrived in downtown Milwaukee on Thursday afternoon. I went to the expo and picked up my number.

The next day, I went to check on my bike. I had it delivered to Milwaukee from TriBike Transport. The bike was in perfect condition, and I went for a little test ride to check on the gears and the new tires I had recently replaced.

I went by the water to go for a test swim, but the water was rough. There was a storm coming, and everyone who jumped in talked about how cold it was. I didn't know if I should go in. I texted my coach. She told me I should and to see if the sleeveless wetsuit worked. I was still reluctant. Then I saw Vicki, who is a local Long Island coach and friend.

"Come on Hilary, we're going in!" she said enthusiastically. If she hadn't pushed me, I don't know if I would have gone.

I put my feet in. The water was ice cold. It felt as if I were putting my feet in an ice bath. I sat on the dock and waited. The woman next to me was having a panic attack about how swimming was her worst discipline. I walked away. I was so nervous I didn't want to think about her worst discipline. I wanted to focus on myself.

I went down the ladder and jumped in. Hey, if I could jump in the Hudson River, I could do anything, right? It was a shock to my body. My feet, arms, and hands were numb. I swam. At first, I didn't want to put my face in, but I forced myself. I swam some more. It was peaceful and beautiful. The water was an amazing greenish-blue color, clear, and it was fresh water.

I went back to the hotel and got ready. I was in panic mode. I got a text from my son, that really put me back on earth. "Did you know that you have a high ranking with USA Triathlon?" he texted. "Well, you do, and you know what, no matter what, I am so proud of you." He made me smile. He always does. That night, I got up every hour. I asked myself, "Is it time yet?"

At 4:30 a.m., I jumped out of bed. My coach told me to be at transition at 6:30 a.m. but I was just too nervous, so I got there a little earlier. I should have listened to her. I set up my transition area but then I had so much time to kill. I sat on the grass and meditated for a while. Everyone was anxious and nervous.

HILARY JM TOPPER

One woman said, "I just hope I can beat someone." I laughed and said, "You can beat me . . ."

I wasn't concerned with beating anyone. I just wanted to enjoy the experience and do what I love to do—swim, bike, run.

When our wave was finally called, I saw Sharon, a friend from Long Island. She gave me a hug and said, "We've got this."

I was intimidated by these amazing athletes. It struck me most in the water. Many took off when the horn blew, and I was swimming alone for a while. It wasn't until the end, when the men caught up, that I started to feel like I was in a race.

The water was freezing but after the first 100 yards, I got used to it. I felt very relaxed, maybe too relaxed. I felt myself glide through the water with my wetsuit and loved the feeling.

Swim Time: 00:46:00

I ran into transition. I could feel the adrenaline. When I stopped running, I felt as if I should keep on running. I'm not sure why I stopped. I got to my bike and most of the bikes in my wave were already out. I didn't let myself think about it. I just had to focus on the moment. I put on my cycling shoes and ran my bike out of transition.

I mounted on the bike and rode. At first, my pedals didn't clip in, and I was nervous I was going to fall. But once I got going, I clipped in, and I was good.

My friend who had done the course before told me that the course was flat. *Flat?* Yes, at first it was flat but at mile 2.5, there was a steep hill that went straight up. Oh boy, that was tough. The other tough part was going on the bridge. I felt as if I was on Harlem Hill x2! (Harlem Hill is the largest hill in Central Park. It's got a 4.4 grade and lasts for more than a quarter mile.)

The course was pleasant. It went through three Milwaukee suburbs. There were plenty of people out cheering.

I kept pushing. The more I rode, the stronger I was feeling, until the end. After I got over the bridge, I asked a volunteer, "Is there much more?" She told me there were two miles left. Then, I was happy! But my butt and legs were burning. I was done with the bike.

124

Bike Time: 1:07:00

Back into transition, I put on my sneakers, my Iron Fit Endurance cap and took off. I had my watch set on a four-minute run/one-minute walk.

On the run, some people passed me, and I passed some people. As people were passing me, they said, "Good work," which was ticking me off at that point. I felt like they were being condescending. They were passing me. It was as if they were saying good work to themselves for passing me.

Some of the spectators shouted go "Iron Fit." And, while I was on my walk breaks, I was getting hassled by some of the runners because I was walking.

The run was gorgeous. The path that ran along the water had breathtaking views. Unfortunately, I didn't get to take it in. Instead, I focused on moving forward. During the run, my knees started to give out. I would get severe pain when I ran and then tried to walk it off.

Suddenly a ninety-two-year-old man passed me. I couldn't believe it. I became inspired. If he could do this, I could too!

About a quarter mile from the finish line, I ran in. I picked up the pace. Not sure what my mental block was, but I had something that was stopping me from going all out the entire time. I crossed the finish line, and I was so happy it was over.

Run Time: 1:25:00

Total Time: 4:10:00

Here were some amazing tweets I received via text and Twitter:

8:01 a.m. "You've got this Hilary!" from Coach Danielle Sullivan, and at 1:49 p.m., she texted me, "You did it!!!!"

"Congratulations! You did it! This was a huge accomplishment. You did great!" from Becky as I finished the race.

"Congratulations to AWTT's very own Hilary Topper. USA National Triathlon in Milwaukee!!!! You make us proud . . ." from Megan White, co-coach of All Women's Tri Team

"So impressed by my mom @hilary25 for competing in the USA Triathlon National Championship today! We're all so proud of your accomplishments!" from Derek

****

Right after Milwaukee, I raced in the Nation's Triathlon in Washington, DC. This time, I jumped into the Potomac River! It was an awesome experience doing it with my friends from AWTT.

Looking back, I realized that although I did a lot of triathlons that year, it helped me grow. The races were exciting and the people I met along the way made it all worth it.

Lesson Learned

In the beginning of the year, pick one or two "A" races that have been on your bucket list. Then add a couple of "B" races and "C" races. Create an Annual Training Plan (ATP) and focus on your "A" races. Don't go overboard and burn yourself out.

2016

"If at any time, you feel overwhelmed or out of control in your life, take a deep breath and volunteer at a triathlon race to be inspired!"
–Noah Lam, Ironman, founder/coach of Lightning Warriors Youth Triathlon Team, New York

CHAPTER 18

Challenge Yourself

During the summer of 2015, as I was competing in all those triathlons, I kept thinking that there needed to be a place to get education about triathlons, but I couldn't find anything.

Throughout my life, whenever I saw a need, I took it upon myself to address that need. That is why I decided to host the NYTRI Expo at Citi Field in March 2016. I got my whole family, my entire staff, all my friends, and my Hofstra students to help coordinate the day.

It was a sensational event with more than 2,000 in attendance, seventy vendors/booths, and more than twenty concurrent seminars teaching registrants everything about triathlon and running including hydration, nutrition, and even injury prevention. I was able to secure two amazing keynote speakers. One was Matt Dixon of Purple Patch Fitness in San Francisco. Matt was a professional triathlete and wrote two incredible books. He was the perfect keynote speaker, so motivating! In addition to that, I honored Matt Long, author and coach, and gave a donation to his charity that helps athletes with disabilities. It was a day I will always remember!

NEW YORK CITY MARATHON

The same month as the expo, I got accepted into the New York City Marathon, I was thrilled. This would be my first full marathon. I couldn't believe it. I had been trying to get in ever since I had started running with Becky. She had run it a few years before we ran together, and I was in awe of her for doing that. She convinced me that I would love it and every year after that, I put my name in the hat.

When I got in, I was a wreck! How can I do this? Where do I start? Having known Jeff Galloway after meeting him at the Tower of Terror race, hosting him on my podcasts, and using him as a regular contributor on my blog, I turned to him. "Jeff, I don't know how to get started," I told him.

"Hilary, it would be my pleasure to train you," he said. And with that, Jeff graciously told me he would take me on as a private client.

"How much will it cost?" I asked him.

"For you, Hilary, nothing."

That was such a good day. Now, I was having an Olympian train me the right way to run with the Run Walk Run method. I knew I would be okay.

I had a ton of work trips and vacations scheduled. My triathlon coach told me to try to either race or run when I traveled. That year, I also did a few small triathlons including Power of a Woman in April, Jamesport Triathlon in July, and Tri the Wildwoods Triathlon in August.

In addition to that, I also did the West Neck Beach Swim—one-mile swim in July.

WEST NECK SWIM

Excel Swimming, the organizers of the West Neck Swim and Master Swimming group, had tons of people in the water watching the swimmers. It was a slow start. My group walked into the water, swam a little to warm up, and then waited by the yellow buoy until the horn went off. As soon as we heard the horn, we started swimming.

Becky was feeling anxious about the swim, many of the AWTT members stayed with her. I really couldn't understand why she was so anxious because I knew she was a strong swimmer. But, as she said to me, "You're not in my head." And obviously that was true.

I started to swim. I wasn't hustling, I was just going. A mile was a long way. Slow and steady, I kept telling myself. I was swimming alongside Megan from AWTT for most of the swim. It felt like the red buoys, the directional buoys, kept appearing. The course was well-marked and great for spotting, one of the best courses I had done up until that point.

I kept having issues with the nose plugs. They kept falling off. I was glad I brought three pairs. I wore them on my fingers. I stopped, adjusted them, and kept on swimming. I tried to be conscious of the kick. Don't kick so hard. Soft kicks, as Danielle would say.

I felt myself glide through the water. I wore my new wetsuit, and I kept my booties on the entire time. They may have held me back a little, but I didn't want to cut up my feet on the North Shore rocks.

I got to the yellow buoy, the turn buoy, at the same time as Megan. I went around it close. I started to swim. She stopped for a moment. I looked over and said, "You, okay?" She nodded, and I kept going. As I was heading back, it felt as if I were the only one in the water. I swam and glided through the water. Every exhale into the water felt exhilarating. The cold water on my face felt good too. I passed a couple of red round buoys and was seeing the yellow buoy. Wait, how could I be seeing a yellow buoy when I'm supposed to see a red one? I picked my head up above the water. OMG, the red buoy was far back! I missed my exit point!

I started to panic. Go faster! I had to turn directions completely. There was no marker to tell you that this was the end. That was upsetting! I was crushed and deflated but pushed forward. I made it to the red buoy and remembered to go right. As I was swimming to shore, I saw Christine, my swimming coach, in the water. "You got this Hilary, you're doing great," she screamed. I could hear my AWTT teammates in the distance, screaming my name. I finally found the chute to exit. Two women pushed their way in front of me. I swam until I couldn't swim any longer. Got up and exited the chute. I could hear the ref saying "fifty-two." Did it take me fifty-two minutes to exit? I thought that was slow for me. I was estimating that I would finish in forty-five minutes.

Overall, I felt good. I felt like I could go another mile. The mile seemed easy to me. A couple of my teammates followed me. I stood and cheered them on. When everyone was in, I walked over to see the results.

At first, I was feeling good, strong, and confident. Then, when the race results came out, I started to doubt myself. Becky, who had the panic attack, ended up coming in faster than me and winning her division. All my teammates came in faster than me. Although I was happy for my teammates, I felt left out.

I started getting in my head. Asking myself the following questions:

- Could I have gone faster?
- What held me back?
- Why did I stop when those swimmers climbed on top of me during the swim? I should have pushed ahead.
- Why did I stop and keep changing the nose plugs?
- Why didn't I see that red buoy? If I did, I would have finished earlier.
- I thought I was a decent swimmer, but obviously, I'm not.
- Can I do anything right?
- Maybe I should drop this sport? I really suck.

Those negative thoughts went on the whole car ride back to my house. I couldn't get them out of my head.

And then I stopped myself.

I took myself back to my first swim at the Long Beach Recreation Center when I attempted to go twenty-five yards but couldn't. Or, when I joined Open Water Swim LI and kept having to stop because I was choking on the water. I've come a long way since those early days, which were less than three years ago. I should be proud of myself. I was proud of myself. I just swam a mile!

I couldn't swim before getting into triathlons. I doggy-paddled, or if I swam for a minute, it was with my head out of the water.

Here, I went a mile, or close to it, in the open water. I felt amazing. I was in my happy place. As I was gliding, I just focused on my stroke and my sightings. I didn't think of anything else, and I felt good about that. So why not focus on that instead of my time or compare myself to others? I was proud of myself, and that's all that matters.

JULY

I've been training for triathlons for nearly three years and every year since I started, I look forward to the day that Bryan announced the Robert Moses swim at sunset.

Open Water Swim LI met on Wednesday evenings in July, an hour before sunset. The sunset swim went from Robert Moses to the Fire Island Lighthouse and back for approximately 1,500 yards.

The swim was tough. If you were lucky, the tide was with you in one direction. It was sometimes nearly impossible to fight the current in the opposite direction.

Thanks to a swimmer friend, Cathy, I learned that the current is just another opportunity to stay longer in the water. "If you think that way, you will get through it . . . just enjoy it," she said.

For the first swim of the season there were at least twenty swimmers. Many of them were practicing for the Cross Bay Swim, which was a 5.5-mile swim in challenging water.

I put on my long-sleeve wetsuit, my bathing cap, my goggles, and walked into the frigid water. Most of the swimmers who walked in with me had already taken off toward the Fire Island Lighthouse. I tried to get acclimated first and then dove in. Once my face got used to it, I felt better and got myself into a rhythm. Before I knew it, I was at Fire Island. Boy, that went fast, I guess the current was with me. The fun part will be going back . . .

Although there was a strong current, it wasn't terrible getting back. I tried to relax and think about what Cathy said. It helped. It's not a race, it's a fun swim in preparation for a race.

As I was coming back, I was blinded by the sun setting in front of me. The bright yellow color illuminated the water and all I saw were flashes of light in front of me.

When I got to the end, there were a bunch of swimmers talking. I stood by them and listened. Then I swam to shore. Interestingly, as I got out of the water, an HJMT vendor was sitting on the sand. I hadn't seen him in a year since he filmed *Glasslandia*, and he was as shocked as I was to see him.

We chatted for a while, and then I spoke with a few other people on the beach. Before I knew it, the sun was low in the horizon, and it was time to go home . . .

Lesson Learned

Some people say to me, I can't get motivated unless I have a race. To me, the training and the whole experience motivates me. It's really about the journey. Think about that for a moment. Think about all the people that you meet along the way. Think about the new friendships. Think about the experience. I always say, "Be grateful."

CHAPTER 19

It's More About the Experience Than the Race

Races aren't just about the race; it is about the whole experience leading up to and after the actual race.

After running the New York Road Runners New York Mini six-miler a few months ago with Zoey, we decided to sign up for the Bronx 10-miler race. This was Zoey's first ten-miler. Since I lived on Long Island, I booked a room at the Days Inn at Yankee Stadium.

"How bad could that be?" I thought.

That Saturday afternoon, I ventured into the city. The traffic was horrible, as usual, and a short ride that should have taken me an hour, took two. As I was on the Grand Central Parkway, I got a low-level tire alert that needed to get adjusted immediately.

I started to panic. Was this a sign? Was someone up there telling me not to do the race?

I went to the gas station on the Grand Central Parkway by LaGuardia Airport and asked the attendant for help. He was gracious and filled all my tires. I was off again.

Now I was late for dinner. Zoey had made a reservation at a nice Italian restaurant by her apartment. I called her and let her know I was running late, very late!

When I finally got there, we had a pasta dinner, went to her apartment, picked up her things and headed into the Bronx.

The warning lights came back on, and I knew there was nowhere to stop at this point, so I kept on going.

Once we arrived at the Days Inn at Yankee Stadium, we parked the car and walked inside to find the receptionist behind a bullet-proof wall. She gave us a room key and we walked into the hotel room to find that we weren't alone!

There was a gigantic cockroach walking on the wall. Not only that, but the fire alarm was going off like crazy! When my daughter complained, the woman behind the bullet-proof wall, came out and walked us down the hall.

The room she put us in was just as bad. It had a perfume scent that tried to cover up the smell of cigarette smoke in the room. When we got there, it took less than two minutes, and I was in the bathroom throwing up.

"Maybe we should leave," my daughter said as I got out of the bathroom.

"No, it will be fine," I said.

She proceeded to check the mattress and bedding for bedbugs. She didn't find any. I turned up the air, and we hesitantly got under the covers to go to bed.

That night, we both tossed and turned. The AC was up so high, we were shivering.

"Boy, you're up a lot," she said to me at 6 a.m. the next morning when we awoke.

I smiled. What was I going to tell her, that I don't sleep?

We dressed and took an Uber to the race. The actual race was uneventful. My daughter was so nervous about this one, and I knew she would do great. I was a little nervous too. Everyone gets nervous before races.

We took off, and I started out slowly with Zoey for the first quarter mile and then went into my coach's recommendation of fifteen-second run–fifteen-second walk and then after mile three, thirty–fifteen. Zoey continued to run the entire ten miles. Impressive!

The race started on the Grand Concourse and went to the Botanical Gardens and back. It was hilly! A few people told us the course was flat. Ha! Zoey screamed out to me at mile five when we were in the park. She was heading in one direction, and I was in the other. It made me smile. I was so proud of her and her accomplishments!

Zoey's boyfriend, Daniel, met us at mile six, which was a godsend! Dan was a guy she met at Syracuse University during Freshman year. He was tall, wore glasses, and, in recent years, kept his hair short. Dan had replacement water bottles for both of us. We ended up finishing the race strong!

AUGUST WILDWOOD TRI

Sometimes you look back on a race and realize that entering it was the wrong decision. Tri the Wildwoods Triathlon in North Wildwood, NJ, was one of those races. I was gearing up for the New York City Marathon and had just gotten back from San Francisco, so I was jetlagged. I had signed up for the IRONMAN 70.3 Atlantic City with Becky. I forked over $400 to the organization. I just wasn't ready, and I couldn't see myself doing something that I wasn't ready to do. As a nice gesture, the race organizer gave me a complementary entry to this race, and I felt compelled to do it. Tri the Wildwoods was an International Triathlon, like an Olympic but slightly shorter. This triathlon consisted of a three-quarters of a mile swim, eighteen-mile bike, and a five-mile run.

My husband joined me, and we drove down to Wildwood. It took us five hours on a Friday afternoon to get there. The traffic was horrendous!

The night before the race, I couldn't sleep as usual. I was nervous. I just wanted to finish, even if I came in last. I was going to enter that finisher chute feeling good about my accomplishments this year.

After getting to transition at 4:45 a.m. when it opened, I set up quickly and started to visualize the race—getting into the water, getting

My mother holding my sister, Lori, and me in a local pool in New York in 1966.

My dad and me running together in South Florida in 2011.

After the NYC Half Marathon in 2012. My son, Derek, ran with me during the last half-mile.

After finishing the Las Olas Triathlon in Ft. Lauderdale, FL, in 2015.

Brian and me biking in Napa, CA, in 2015.

Riding my road bike during the USA National Championship in 2015.

My daughter, Zoey, and me at the NYRR Mini 6-Miler in New York in 2016.

Coach Danielle and me at the Jamesport Triathlon in 2016.

Holding my NYC Marathon medal in 2016.

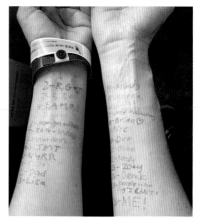

During the 2016 NYC Marathon, I dedicated each mile to someone.

The conclusion of the 2016 NY Tri Expo. My committee members gave me an award which is still in my office today!

Ray and me finishing the
EventPower LI Smithpoint
Triathlon in 2017.
This was Ray's first tri after
I convinced him to "try."

Finishing the Suffolk Half in
a Nor'Easther in 2017.
*Photo courtesy of Greater Long Island
Running Club and Island Photo*

Doing the signature pose in the Amalfi Coast in Italy in 2018.

Running on Jones Beach during leg 1 of the 50K Ultra Relay in 2018.
Photo by Ed Grenzig of LIRP Long Island Running Photos

Coming out of the water at the EventPower LI Smithpoint Triathlon in 2018.
Photo by Ed Grenzig of LIRP Long Island Running, courtesy of EventPower LI

(left to right) Ray, Merril, me, and Colleen placing at EventPower LI Stepping Stone 5K Running Race in Great Neck, NY, in 2018.

At the NYRR Bronx 10 Miler at Yankee Stadium in 2019.

Jeff Galloway and me having a blast on Long Island in 2019.

Joanne and me running the Fall Foliage Race in 2019.

Ray and me in the open water at Tobay Beach in New York in 2020.

Derek took a photo of me streamlining in the pool in Garden City, NY, in 2020.

Running along a dock at Tobay Marina on Long Island, NY, in 2021.

At Tobay Beach on Long Island, NY, in 2021.

On my TT Bike during a training session in 2021.

Boy, this couch potato sure has a lot of medals. I'm proud of all my accomplishments!

Receiving the Endurance Award for finishing the Maggie Fischer Memorial Cross Bay Swim from Fire Island to Bay Shore, Long Island, 2021.

My group, WeREndurance, and me being goofy after training in 2021.

The 2022 Rock 'n' Roll Las Vegas Marathon with the WeREndurance Team.

on the bike, getting to the run. I was nervous. I was trying to "control my mind" and focus on the positive things, like how the race would make me feel during and after completion.

As I was walking toward the beach for the swim start, I met a woman from a New Jersey tri team. She also wore nose plugs, so we started comparing notes about the good plugs and the bad ones. She said she felt bad about wearing them, but they were the only way she could breathe in the water. I told her I felt the same way.

When we got to the water, we parted ways.

I tried to stay calm and focused. I knew what needed to be done.

We entered a corral on the beach for a running start into the water. The men went first about fifteen minutes later than originally planned because the organizers were working with volunteers to get cars off the bike course.

The men ran about a half mile on the beach, into the rough Atlantic Ocean. As soon as the last man was at the yellow buoy, the women were queued to start. The sand was soft and got a little harder as you went toward the water. It had a silky-smooth texture, almost like talcum powder.

I walked. I wasn't going to run on that sand. I was gearing up for the NYC Marathon and the last thing I wanted was to get injured. All fifty women entered the water. I didn't get in until everyone was swimming toward the first buoy.

As I walked into the water, the waves were furiously breaking as I was trying to get to the yellow buoy. I started to do Tarzan. I couldn't catch my breath. The lifeguard saw me and came over. "Hold on to the kayak until you breathe normally," he said.

I was feeling a little frustrated. Should I just quit now?

I put my head in the water and got into a rhythm. Once I was in a rhythm, I could have kept going for miles, and I didn't want to get out. I was really enjoying the swim. I found it so incredibly meditative. I took a few strokes, sighted, took another few strokes, sighted, and kept making my way forward. I loved the way my body bobbed up and down with the waves.

When I got to the third yellow buoy, it was time to exit. There were a lot of people struggling. They were holding on to the lifeguards' surfboard and buoys.

As soon as they saw me, they started to swim. I knew this because at every race, I find that this happens. People wait and then when someone comes, they go for it. I found myself getting tangled with three other women who were kicking and punching me.

The run from the beach to the transition area was at least a quarter mile on the soft sand. Again, I walked. I tried to run, but it was very difficult.

I got to transition, pulled off my wetsuit, and put on my helmet, cycling shoes, and CamelBak. Then I unracked the bike, and I was out. The people at the bike mounting and unmounting station were a little intense. "Don't get on your bike." "Get on your bike." "You lost your gel, WAIT." The man handed me my gel, and I was off.

The bike course wasn't as easy as I thought it would be. There were tons of technical turns. They were sharp at points, and I thought I was going to fall off the bike. And, then there was a very, very steep bridge. I saw this bridge coming into town when Brian and I drove in, but I didn't think it would be on the course. Of course, it was. I had to go over the bridge four times! It was steep and difficult, but I kept telling myself, it's just a little bit further.

There were lots of athletes getting off their bikes and walking. I wasn't going to do that. I knew that was an option, but I wouldn't allow myself to get off because of the time constraints. I kept pushing and pedaling along. Then there was the fast downhill.

That was where I thought I was going to get into an accident. People were braking. One woman in particular kept braking and taking up the entire lane. I shouted, "On your left," and instead of getting over, she went in front of me. As I swerved not to get into an accident, she said, "Oh, sorry."

I was glad the bike section was almost finished because I just couldn't do that bridge yet another time.

As I was approaching the dismount, I slowed down. The man who gave me my gel on the way out stood in front of me. "Dismount now," he said. I almost ran him over! I was startled. "You need to dismount before the white line, it's the rule," he told me. Wow, this guy was way too much!

I ran into transition and saw Brian taking photos. He was standing there waving to me. It made me smile. I was happy he was there. I quickly put on my sneakers and my cap and ran to the other end of transition in the sand.

The run out was onto the beach, and the beach was set back from the boardwalk. When you stood on the boardwalk you couldn't see the water. It was that far away. The sand was soft, and I thought that this would end soon. It didn't. It just kept getting worse. Although for most of the three miles of run on the beach, the sand was packed down; there were sections where you needed to run on the soft sand. I was feeling frustrated. Lots of people were walking, but they were the sprint people, and their run was barely a mile on the beach.

Once I passed the sprint exit, I continued. I saw a half dozen people going in the opposite direction. I thought about bowing out at that point. Maybe I should just turn around with them? But I didn't. I couldn't do that. I wouldn't feel good about myself if I cheated in a race. I would probably feel 100 times worse than I did at that moment. I kept going to the end where the turnaround was on the soft sand and a ton of young children asked me if they could throw water at me. I said, "Umm, no thank you." I took their water and dumped it on my head instead.

"You're doing great," the adult volunteers were saying to me. I knew at that point that I must be the last person because there was no one behind me.

"I feel like I'm the only one on the course," I said.

They laughed and said, "Yes, we created the event just for you." I smiled.

I couldn't run what I expected to run. I started with thirty seconds running–fifteen seconds walking and couldn't do that, so I dropped it to a fifteen/fifteen. That was much more doable in the sand. And, even when I finally got to the boardwalk in the extreme heat, I found that the fifteen/fifteen worked best. It put me at a 14:40 minute per mile, but I didn't care. I was exhausted from running on the sand.

On the boardwalk, I went through two piers that had amusement rides on them. At the point that I was running on the boardwalk, there were tons of people on the course. One of the volunteers apologized to me. "We just couldn't keep it clear," he said. "I'm really sorry."

I couldn't talk, so I just smiled.

The volunteers were very encouraging even though I knew I was the last person to finish the international distance. There were about a dozen or so people behind me who were doing the sprint, but that didn't make me feel any better. I appreciated the volunteers' enthusiasm.

I always thought that the world would end, and I would never do another triathlon again if I came in dead last. At this triathlon, I was the last to finish in the international division. But you know what? The world didn't cave in, no one cared, and I finished the race.

I got a text from my daughter that read:

"You did it and I'm proud of you. You did amazing, no matter how fast you finished."

And from my son: *"You finished it!"* I also got a text message from my sister, my coach, and from my brother, all congratulating me.

And you know what, I was proud of myself. This was a PR on an international race.

I could have backed out at least three times during this race, which took me three hours to complete and yet, I kept telling myself, I need to cross the finish line no matter what. Brian was here to see me. I wanted him to be proud of me. And he was.

Lesson Learned

If you compete in a race and come in dead last, it's okay. The world doesn't end. You still did it, and that's what counts!

CHAPTER 20

New York City Marathon

My "A" race for the year was the New York City Marathon, and although I did other races throughout the year, I always kept my focus on this race. I built up my training for this one by running an additional mile every other week during my long runs until I was up to nine miles.

NINE-MILE RUN

During my nine-mile run, I started thinking about my mother. I never did come to terms with her death, and we had so many unresolved issues.

When my mother got older, the polio came back. She had post-polio syndrome, a disorder that many polio victims got in their later years. The post-polio slowly debilitated her and toward the end, she could no longer walk. She needed a scooter to get around. She could no longer breathe on her own without the use of oxygen, 24/7. She fought it. She didn't want to use the scooter. She didn't want to use the oxygen. She didn't want anyone to see her weakness. But toward the end, it got the better of her.

I started running only a couple of years before my mother passed away. She used to tell me I was crazy for running such distances. She would worry that I would get hurt. But I didn't listen. I loved the sport and kept on doing it.

Whenever I visited her in Florida, I would get up early and run around her complex. I would see her looking out the window watching me. I knew she secretly wished she could do it too.

While I was running a nine-mile run on the Wantagh Parkway path, I started to think about why I run, and I realized that I run for my mother. I run because my mother couldn't. I run because of all those people who can't.

I run because I can.

RUNNING THIRTEEN MILES

A couple of weeks later, my training plan was to run thirteen miles. I didn't want to run thirteen miles. Still, I strategized for days prior to the run. How should I do this?

For starters, my coach reminded me to keep hydrated. "Even if you think you are hydrated, drink more," she told me.

Two weeks before, I ran eleven miles and got very sick, I took her advice to heart. I was also suffering from an Achilles problem. She recommended I see a chiropractor.

Achilles tendonitis is a common injury among runners. When it flares up, the pain is so intense it can stop you in your tracks. Between the chiropractor and the kinesiology tape, I was able to keep training.

I decided to run seven miles to Point Lookout, the next town over, and back to Lido Beach. It felt so good. I was feeling happy, relaxed, and really enjoying the run and the scenery. It was gorgeous in Point Lookout. Some of the homes were magnificent, and you were only steps away from the water. When I was at the end of the Point, I looked out and saw the sun rising over the water. I smiled. I looked out and could see Jones Beach and what I thought looked like Fire Island. I started to think about all the people swimming the 5.5-miles in the Cross Bay event. I was rooting for them!

I made my way back to Lido Beach, circled around the middle school before returning to my house for a quick bathroom break and restock of my hydration. I took a couple of dollars out of my bag, just in case

I wanted something on the boardwalk, and ran out the door. I was still feeling pretty good.

I took a water bottle and stashed it in the weeds by Lido Towers. I figured I could use it later.

At mile nine, my Achilles started to flare up. I had a burning sensation around my leg leading into the Achilles. I was in horrible pain. I didn't know what to do. If I went back, I wouldn't have completed my goal of thirteen miles, and if I went forward, I wouldn't have been able to walk.

I went over to the man pulling two containers of ice cream. "Do you have a chunk of ice I can buy?" I asked him.

"No but ask that girl over there behind the ice cream truck," he said.

I went over to her to ask the same question. She opened the ice cream hatch and said, "Nope, I have nothing for you."

I told her to look in the large cooler.

She looked over at the guy I originally asked for approval. He shook his head, and she went into the cooler and took out one small ice cube. It was ridiculous. I didn't offer her money. I thanked her and sat on the bench and iced my Achilles. I started to cry from the pain. I wished I had brought Advil with me.

The ice lasted a minute, literally, and I started to do twenty–thirty on the run–walk. I had to force myself to continue. I only had another mile or so before I had to turn around to complete the thirteen miles.

I kept going. I pushed myself forward. I saw a little restaurant on the boardwalk. I stopped and asked for ice. This time, the woman was gracious and gave me a quarter cup of ice.

I hobbled over to the bench and iced away. I just wished the pain would dissipate. After sitting for another couple of minutes. I got up and continued.

Finally, I got to the end of the route and was able to turn around. I started to run. The running felt easier than the walking.

I saw four police officers talking. I asked if they had Advil. "Nope, but maybe the female one over there has some," the officer said.

I went to the female officer. She didn't have any either. Why didn't I bring Advil with me?

I headed back. I debated on whether to call a friend or call a taxi. I didn't do either. I forced myself to continue because I needed to get in the miles. If I quit at that moment, I would have questioned whether I could do the full marathon, which was 26.2 miles. If I couldn't do thirteen miles, how could I do 26.2 miles? I was at mile twelve now, with only one mile to go.

I circled around the Lido Beach Towers and found the water bottle I hid in the grass. I poured it on my head. Too bad I didn't bring ice!

I kept going. The pain was unbearable, but I mentally couldn't stop. Tears were streaming down my face because it hurt so bad. I finally reached my house and circled the area before going home.

****

TWENTY-MILE RUN IN MASSAPEQUA

As my training picked up, I wanted to run somewhere different. A Facebook friend suggested I run Massapequa Preserve to Bethpage State Park, up to the Syosset train station. He said it was about ten miles each way. So, I decided to give it a shot!

Massapequa was on the south shore of Long Island. The Preserve was gorgeous. It was set away from traffic, and although from time to time you saw homes, you felt like you were running in the country. There were lots of trees, babbling brooks, ducks, and interesting birds there.

I parked my car by Linden Boulevard and went north. The first ten miles were uneventful. I listened to my music, drank from my CamelBak marathon hydration pack, and just felt the warmth and beauty of the park. I was feeling a little unsure of myself, never having been there before, so from time to time, I would ask people if I were going in the right direction.

At mile thirteen, I started to hurt. I had seven miles to go, and I already felt pain in my hips, my legs, my feet, my back, you name it, I felt the pain! I took two to three minutes out and stretched. I did this a few more times during those last seven miles.

At mile sixteen, I was ready to quit. I was back at my car and saw that Coach Danielle had tagged me on Facebook. She wrote:

"First twenty-miler in six years in the books! Thank you Salty, the dog, for helping me ice my legs! Hope your twenty-miler is going great, too, Hilary Topper!"

That motivated me. How can I stop? I told my entire family and friends that I was going to do twenty miles and how will I feel if I only do sixteen? And now this post.

I ran south this time from my car on Linden Boulevard. The southern part of the trail was even more beautiful than the northern part. I passed a group of young women running for school. I passed people fishing. I even passed a bunch of ducks in the water. "I can do this," I kept telling myself. "I need to work through this pain and keep going!"

I wrote to my coach: "I'm not going to be able to do this." Then I wrote back, "Can I take a rest?" And then finally, and I can only imagine what she was thinking at this point, I wrote again, "I am going to get this done!"

And that's what I did . . . I was so happy that I forced myself to finish and fight through the pain. At that moment, I knew I would be able to get through the marathon.

After the twenty miles, I drank a couple of cosmopolitan cocktails, went into my massage chair, went in the hot tub, took a hot bath with mineral salt, and put lots of band-aids on my feet to cover all the blisters. Next stop, twenty-three miles—oh no!

TWENTY-THREE MILES

It was a cold, dreary day. The dark clouds suggested that it might rain at any moment. I was prepared. Earlier in the week, I went to a few of the stores in Roosevelt Field Shopping Center and was scrambling to find a waterproof jacket. I finally found one at Dick's Sporting Goods in the men's department, and I bought it.

I wore my long-sleeve running shirt over a tank top and put the jacket on before I went out. I was prepared for my route. My son, Derek, helped me figure it out.

My plan:
- Run from Lido Beach to the Atlantic Beach Bridge
- Run the Long Beach Boardwalk twice
- Run home, restock my water bottles, and head to Point Lookout for a short six-mile run.

I put on my hydration system and was out the door by 8 a.m. Jeff Galloway suggested that I do an easy run of ten–fifty (run–walk ratio). I was going to stick with that ratio until I was at mile eleven, and then I was going to do ten–forty, and then five miles out at ten–thirty.

Everything was going as planned. As I was running, I started to get emotional. I started to think about the people in my life and how grateful I was!

I thought about my mother and how she had so much trouble walking her entire life, and here I was running twenty-three miles. She would have been either proud or thinking I am out of my mind!

But my kids were my true inspiration. Knowing that they were rooting for me made me want to do this.

I ran back through the west end area of Long Beach without a hitch. It was Irish Day, a huge annual festival. I thought I may get caught up, but all I bumped into were teens on their bikes riding with six packs of beer. I ran toward Atlantic Beach. I was never over that way before. Who goes to Atlantic Beach when living in Long Beach? The only time I drove through there was to go to the airport over the Atlantic Beach Bridge. But this time, I ran to the bridge.

Then I did something I have never done. I ran on the Atlantic Beach Boardwalk. I didn't even know there was a boardwalk there! The Atlantic

Beach Boardwalk is nice, but it only spans one mile in each direction, unlike the Long Beach boardwalk that runs 2.1 miles each way.

I ran back through the west end and saw more kids with beer. One kid almost ran me over . . . that was scary!

When I got back on the boardwalk, I got to the end and then turned around. I needed four more miles to get this right. As I was running along, my watch battery light went on. I immediately texted my coach, "What should I do?"

She said, "You'll just have to run without it . . ." But she helped me troubleshoot the situation. That put a damper on my run. I loved seeing the mileage when I finished. It stopped at fourteen miles.

I put on two apps on my iPhone—RunGo and MapMyRun. I figured one of them would be accurate. I ran another 3.5 miles back to my house. There, I planned to replenish my water bottles but instead, I was hurting. I took off my sneakers and socks and replaced them with new ones. I realized the jacket I bought was wrong for running. It didn't breathe! I took off my tights and put on shorts. I was sweating. I was overdressed. I had five miles left and decided to do it on the treadmill.

The next 3.5 miles I ran and walked a little on the treadmill. I kept it on a low jog. At 3.6 miles, I started to get a severe pain in my toe. It felt as if someone was trying to break it off. I stopped. I was done. Twenty-one miles instead of twenty-three.

I felt disappointed that I didn't complete what my running coach told me to do, but I was also glad I was able to get most of it done.

NOVEMBER—THE BIG DAY

Weeks leading up to the New York City Marathon were both emotionally and physically stressful.

The day before the event, my husband and I stayed in the city because the day of the marathon, I needed to be at the Marriott Marquis in Times Square at 6 a.m. I talked him into staying with me, which he wasn't thrilled about.

"What am I going to do when you run by?" he said. Since my kids wanted to be there, he decided to join them.

That night, I tossed and turned, just as I do with other major races. I had a dream about a dog. I'm not sure whose dog it was, but the dog kept jumping off the roof and landing on its feet. I woke up thinking the dog must be me.

I got up at 4:45 a.m., dressed and mixed my nutritional supplements and was out the door by 5:30 a.m. As I walked over to the Marriott from the Bryant Park Hotel where I was staying, I was surprised to see so many people on the streets, including marathon runners. They were all headed toward the buses.

Once on the bus, it took us directly to the drop-off location in Staten Island. When we got there, we stood in a long line to go through security. After that, it was smooth sailing. I paid for the VIP access, because I was so nervous. I immediately found the white tent on the right and went in. It was nice and heated! I found a chair and I sat, and I waited nearly three hours before taking off. During that time, I was getting texts, emails, and messages of encouragement. My cousin, Hal, called me and wished me luck. "You got to win this thing," he said. I laughed. Hopefully, I will finish!

I had a plan to run fifteen-minute miles the entire way. A marathon is a long distance, and I was afraid to burn myself out. I chose the fifteen-second run and thirty-second walk and stuck with that the entire race.

For emotional support along the run, I decided to dedicate every mile to someone who made an impact on my life and wrote it on my arm with an indelible marker.

At 10:15 a.m., I made my way out to the cold and the crowds. There, I tried to position myself in the front of my pace group. I knew that the course would be closed after a certain point, and I wanted to make it into the park before then.

I had a last-minute pit stop and got back in the pack. We inched our way up the ramp to the Verrazano Bridge. The national anthem was sung for the fourth time and a cannon went off. We started running. I was a little afraid that my fifteen–thirty would be detrimental to my race because of the other runners, but to my pleasant surprise, most of the folks in the last wave were doing the same thing that I was doing—a run–walk of some sort. Many people were walking up the bridge. I felt confident and strong. It was the first time in a long time that I felt good.

The bridge was not bad, even if it was a mile going uphill. That first mile, I dedicated to my sister, Lori, and her boyfriend, John. Mile two was a downhill from the Verrazano Bridge into Brooklyn. That mile I dedicated to my brother-in-law, Gary, sister-in-law, Rebecca, and nephew, Jeffrey.

Brooklyn was an exciting borough. There were lots of people on the streets. It was cool going through different neighborhoods and seeing the signs along the way. It was an election year, and Donald Trump was running against Hillary Clinton. There were so many signs in Brooklyn that read, "Run fast so that Trump doesn't grab your pussy," with a photo of a cat, and "Run as if you were running for president because anyone could." There were mostly pro-Hillary signs, although I did see one or two pro-Trump signs in Manhattan.

Miles three through fourteen were incredible. I felt fantastic. I had a big smile on my face and thought about the following people:

Mile three—Stefanie, Joe, and Finley (my niece and nephew just had a beautiful baby, Finley)

Mile four—Ed, Andrea, Max, Ben, and Jacob (my brother, sister-in-law, and nephews)

Mile five—Sharon and Zoe (my sisters-in-law)

Mile six—Marilyn and Stan (my mother-in-law and father-in-law)—Marilyn was one of the strongest women I knew who has built an incredible business, and Stanley was the most amazing father! He reminded me of one of the TV dads, always there for his kids!

Mile seven—Rose and Irving (my paternal grandparents)—Although they passed several years before, my grandmother was my rock. She always listened to me and was there for me. My grandfather was encouraging, too. He was the one who told me to "reach for the stars" and I always did.

At that point, I saw Zoey holding up a sign reading: *"You are my hero, Hilary Topper"*.

It was so nice to see her, my husband, and Dan. They were amazing. They kept refilling my water bottles with hydration and providing me with gels.

Mile eight—Max and Ann (my maternal grandparents)—How I loved these two people so much! They were so incredibly loving and, although my grandmother was always sick, she always shared her love with her family. My grandfather was also incredible. We started a dog walking business until, one day, a dog bit us both!

Mile nine—HJMT—I started HJMT with nothing, knowing nothing about business but knowing everything about getting publicity for clients. I had so many obstacles. Curve balls constantly thrown my way and yet, twenty-five years later, we still survived.

Mile ten—New York Road Runners' coaches—I was grateful for the virtual program.

Mile eleven—Dan (my daughter's boyfriend)

Mile twelve—My dad—He was one of the most persistent people I knew and was able to get stuff done.

Mile thirteen—Lisa—I loved working with her. She was such a good friend.

Mile fourteen—Mindy—We grew up together and were close as sisters

At mile fourteen, I saw the Citigroup Center in Queens. There was Zoey, Dan, and Brian again, waiting to refill my bottles! I was feeling great.

When I left them and before I went on the 59th Street Bridge, I saw my friend Wendy, manning the water booth. She ran with me for a few minutes, and we chatted. It was great seeing her on the course!

That gave me a little boost to go up the 59th Street Bridge, but between the wind and the steepness of the bridge, I started to walk. My chest was bothering me. I was finding it hard to breathe. I gave myself a squirt with my inhaler but that didn't really help. I was a little concerned that I may need to stop because the pain was intense. So, I walked.

Mile fifteen—Jessica (my sister's youngest daughter)—She always brought a smile to my face.

Mile sixteen—Ruth (my therapist) who had helped me by digging deep into my past.

As we ran off the bridge into Manhattan, I thought I would hear the roar of the crowds, but instead, it was quiet. Everyone already left and yet, there were 10,000-plus people behind me. I was excited to be back in my old neighborhood!

As I approached 81st Street, I saw my family again. I swapped out the bottles, talked with them for a minute or two and was off. I was excited to enter the Bronx!

I started to notice the people around me like the juggling Forrest Gump for president, or the three British women wearing only sparkling bras, or the woman wearing a superhero cape. There was also an older man, George, who was in his eighties, running by. In addition, there were tons of women running for "two." It was so cool to see all these people experiencing the same thing that I was experiencing.

Mile seventeen—Jeff Galloway—He's been training me for this marathon for several months and I appreciated his feedback. He helped me to love running again. I could not have done this marathon without him.

Mile eighteen—Brian, my husband—As we were still in Manhattan, I dedicated this mile to Brian. I met him when I was twelve, and since then we've been best friends. Although he gets mad at me for doing these "crazy" things, like signing up for a marathon, in the end, he always supports my decision and for that, I dedicated this mile to him.

Mile nineteen—New York City—I love New York City. I've had my most memorable times in that city and running the streets of the five boroughs was an incredible experience!

I left Manhattan and went over the Third Avenue bridge. As we were running, the police came by and said that "this was the end of the police escort" and that we needed to stay on the sidewalk if we wanted to complete the race. It was only five hours into the race. I really couldn't believe it. People around me were angry. They traveled from Sweden and England to race, and they were not going on the sidewalk.

Going over the bridge into the Bronx, I stayed on the bike path with many others. As we got closer to the end, we had to jump over a fence to get back to the road! It was ridiculous. I could barely climb up the fence, and one of the women in the sparkling bras helped me over it. That was nice!

Mile twenty—Coach Danielle—Mile twenty has been my hardest mile throughout my training. I did it twice and couldn't make it farther. Danielle had been so encouraging during the entire training, and the day before, she called me after her big Ironman Florida race to tell me that it was okay if I needed more walk breaks. Knowing that made me feel better.

As I ran the streets of the Bronx, I saw two of my teammates from the AWTT. They were handing out oranges to the runners. I stopped, gave them both hugs, and went on my way.

Mile twenty-one—Gino (my sister's vicious dog)—This little pup was cute and cuddly but never get too close. I had been bitten more than once! I knew that twenty-one would be tough, and the thought of Gino chasing after me pulled me through!

Now, I crossed over another bridge into Manhattan on the west side. I knew that my family would be there. I was excited to see them. I got a jolt of energy. And, when I saw them, I opted out of getting more gels or hydration. "I think I'm actually going to do this!" I screamed out to them as I passed by.

My daughter screamed back, "You got this, ma . . ."

At the same time, I got a text from Derek, who was away at UC Berkeley in California, "You can do it Mom, I know you can."

I pushed on.

Mile twenty-two—Mom—I started to think about my mom. I wore her "P" angel pin, on my shirt. I started to cry. I miss her so much! She had so much adversity in her life from the time she was a little girl, between polio, asthma, and COPD. Although she was always sick, she persevered and loved life.

I kept going. There was a hill on Fifth Avenue and then into the park for another tough hill. Fifteen/thirty, I kept telling myself. "You can do this," I said out loud.

Mile twenty-three and mile twenty-four—Zoey and Derek—They are my life. They are the best thing that ever happened to me and, thankfully, they were so supportive of the things that I did. Every day, I thank God for giving them to me. I cried some more.

The last three miles were torturous. We were now running in complete darkness. Everyone around me was walking. I ran–walked. I wasn't going to stop, although I did realize that they walked much faster than me when I ran. I just caught up and then fell back. I felt like this would never end. It was cold and dark, and I was afraid my music would give out. "Battery low," I heard in my ears.

Mile twenty-five—People who say they can't—There are so many people in my life who say that, but it's not true. You can do whatever you set your mind to do, just like my grandfather once told me. If you want to run a marathon, do it! You got this in you!

We ran past Columbus Circle and back into the park. We were getting close, and I was feeling excited. The last mile, mile twenty-six, was for me, for all the curve balls and the struggles I endured every day and for my accomplishments. I started to think about my life and, much like my mom's life, nothing came easy. I guess going through all of that made me a stronger person so when someone tells me I can't, I always want to prove them wrong.

As I saw the finish line and, thankfully, people were still there giving out medals, I was getting very emotional. I saw Brian, Zoey, and Dan screaming my name, cheering me on. I started to cry. I really got this.

This was a goal that I wanted to achieve for many years, for as long as I could remember. I got this and as I crossed the finish line, I got a call on my mobile phone.

"Mom, you did it! I'm so proud of you." It was Derek on the other end. I was weeping now. I had never had such an amazing experience, and it was so incredibly emotional. I felt bad that I was crying but I couldn't help myself. Between my husband being there, Zoey and Dan cheering me on and helping me with the replacements, and Derek's words of encouragement, I began to think how grateful I am for my family, friends, and all the people in my life who have supported me, because while nothing ever came easy, I never quit fighting, and finishing this Marathon was an example of that!

Lesson Learned

When you race an endurance race, you have a lot of time with yourself to think about things. Try to focus on the people who have helped you in your journey. Dedicating every mile to people who meant something to me was important. It helped me to get through the race. I know you will find it beneficial, too!

2017

"It's going to hurt you. Know it's going to hurt. You didn't train so it wouldn't hurt. You trained so you can take the hurt and still continue ..."

–Dave Murcott, Ironman, New York

CHAPTER 21

On Giving Back

In 2017, I focused on giving back. Jeff Galloway helped me become a marathoner. I wanted to help him and others by teaching the Galloway method. I also wanted to start a group because I wanted to see if there were others like me who were dealing with adversity and needed an outlet.

JANUARY

After the marathon, I asked Jeff if I could start a running group on Long Island. I went through a rigorous training at the end of the year and spoke with his entire staff. I decided that I would have a kickoff in January after I came back from Florida.

I booked my flight to see my dad and thought I should also run the Miami Half (which was part of the Miami Marathon). I was still in good condition from the marathon. Heck, after the marathon, I went out to dinner with my family instead of crashing for endless days or weeks. The run–walk method really works.

The timing was perfect. When I went down to Florida, I met my dad and we both went to the Miami Marathon Expo to pick up my number and check out the vendors. It was a huge expo—just as big as the NYC Marathon expo!

My dad and I walked around and had such a great time. He loved it. I was just afraid that he would get lost. His Alzheimer's disease was starting to get worse; he was still aware but very forgetful. I decided to keep him home while I raced Miami because I didn't want him to be alone.

The next evening, I kissed my dad and I headed down to Miami. I checked into the InterContinental Hotel, which was not too far to the start line and very close to the finish line.

That morning, I woke up at 4:30 a.m., put on my clothes, and walked to the start line. I had heard it may rain so I went with dad the day before to get a raincoat and hat from Dick's Sporting Goods.

The organizers wanted us to get to the start line by 5 a.m. for a 6 a.m. start.

I stood in line and, as usual, met some amazing people. All fifty states were represented at this marathon/half marathon, and there were athletes from dozens of countries. I met a woman from Miami Beach who told me about her running group and all her marathon experiences, and I also met a woman from Fort Lauderdale, running her first half.

As we stood there, 6 a.m. came and went. The people with disabilities went first, then each corral was grouped in five-minute intervals. By the time my group started the race, it was nearly 7 a.m. It was raining hard and freezing. The rain didn't let up and, thankfully, there were runners giving out garbage bags to everyone to shield themselves from the rain.

The rain was pouring down from the sky as we approached the start line. I was still so close to my hotel, "If I could sneak away, I could go back to the hotel and go back to bed," I thought.

I struggled with myself, and I saw others struggling too. But we were slammed into the start line like sardines and there really wasn't a way out.

We must all have looked so funny, running with the garbage bags! At some point, I couldn't stand mine any longer and discarded it. Even though I had bought a jacket, I was soaked!

As we ran, the rain let up a little, but for most of the run it drizzled. We ran over several bridges and saw the cruise ships lined up with people outside cheering us on. We ran through the gorgeous neighborhoods of Miami Beach and South Beach. During most of the run, you saw water, which I loved seeing.

At mile one, I had to go to the bathroom. I stood in line for five minutes to use the porta-potties and then decided to keep moving forward. At mile three, I saw the line was so long but then I saw bushes. Okay, okay, when you gotta go, you gotta go! And anyway, if the men could do it, I can do it too!

I finished the Miami Half strong, feeling good, and even had a PR!

STARTING A RUN-WALK GROUP

When I got back from Miami, I put out a call on Facebook. I knew from my own personal experience that if someone else started this group up I would have joined, no questions asked! After meeting Jeff at a runDisney event, I was enamored. I wanted to learn his method, and fast! But it's not that simple. Run-Walk-Run can take a while to master.

I was pleasantly surprised at how many people were interested. We started with a group of twenty and met every Saturday and some Sundays from February through May. After that, we went on a yearly program. We had some of the coldest, most brutal days to train, but we all were out there. If I didn't have this obligation, I would have stayed in bed most of those days. So, I'm grateful to the group for getting me out of bed!

We met on the Long Beach Boardwalk, Cedar Creek Park, Heckscher Park, Massapequa Preserve, and other places on Long Island. I tried to change it up each week to make it interesting.

I have some great memories of this first group. For starters, the runs were incredible, and the people were even better! I was so inspired by everyone. Dawn, for example, was one of the members from the original group. It was also her first day of radiation treatment for breast cancer. I was blown away by her determination.

We ran our first magic mile as a group. The magic mile was a way to measure your run–walk time by running the track four times, making up a mile. The first quarter mile, you go out easy, second time a little harder, third time even harder, and fourth time an all-out effort. Once I had the numbers, I inputted them into a spreadsheet, and I was able to figure out what run–walk ratio each person should do during training and racing.

We had a couple of our runners do a nine-minute mile. When we did our second one six weeks later, one person came in at 7:40, and another did an 8:15-minute mile! Everyone else who did it the second time, improved by at least thirty seconds. I think this convinced everyone the program works.

The best part for me was when the team ran our first 5K together at the Long Island Marathon.

Many of the people had never run a mile, no less a 5K! Seeing them all cross the finish line brought tears to my eyes. I was so incredibly proud of them.

We held a little after party after the race, where everyone received a beautiful medal. I was so psyched after that that I decided to go for a swim to end the perfect day!

Following that race, we competed in an NYCRUNS Ice Cream Social race on Roosevelt Island. We had a ton of people attend, and it was a total blast.

We wanted to go the distance and train for a half marathon, so many of us signed up for the Suffolk Half Marathon and we started to train.

Training went slow. We built up the mileage every other week until we got to fourteen miles.

AUGUST AND RUNNING FOURTEEN MILES IN THE RAIN

We met at Heckscher State Park because it has a large four-mile loop. It started to rain. "Oh, it's not that bad," I thought. "It will clear up."

It didn't clear up. It poured, and we were all wearing the wrong clothing. We ran anyway.

We started with seven. After the first loop, two runners decided to stop. After the second loop, a few more members dropped and, when we finally finished, we were down to three.

There's something special about running in the rain with such a great group of people. I really felt like we bonded more because we experienced this together. During the run, we joked, laughed, and even cried. When we stopped at the porta-potties, we found our clothing stuck to our skin, it was that wet!

Our first lap, we noticed that Juvenile Diabetes Research Foundation (JDRF) was having their walk.

On our third lap, when there were just three people left, Colleen, who through this running experience became a good friend, Emily, and me, crossed the JDRF finish line, and the crowds were cheering. Since they were so nice to us, I decided to send in a donation.

I've learned that when you organize a running group, you obviously don't do this for the money; you do it because you love to give back and help mentor people. Somewhat self-servingly, I also did it to get myself out the door on a weekend morning. Still, I met an amazing group of people who were inspiring and motivating and have become my running family.

RUNNING THE SUFFOLK COUNTY HALF MARATHON IN A NOR'EASTER

The threat of a Nor'easter kept us skeptical. However, five members of our running team rose to the occasion and ran 13.1 miles in the torrential downpour!

This was a turning point race for me. My friends on Facebook suggested that I try to PR every race. Before this, I wasn't pushing myself enough. So, in this race, I wanted to have a PR, and I knew I could do it. I just needed to push.

I picked up Merrill, one of my runners, at about 6 a.m. We drove to Patchogue together. We were looking for the "Verizon" lot because the race organizers told the runners to park there. At first, we couldn't find it.

We circled once and then turned around and saw cars lining up. We were the third car there!

The volunteer told us to pull up on the lawn. I said to Merrill, "This is going to be a problem when we come back, just you see."

As we were collecting our running gear, Colleen approached us. She was happy to see us, and we were glad to see her too!

The rain was getting heavy. We loaded on shuttle buses to the starting point at the local YMCA. When we arrived, we rushed over to the ladies' room but there was a huge line. We were told there was a private restroom down the hall. We followed some of the other runners. There was no line.

The building was incredibly crowded. It felt as if we were on 42nd Street in Manhattan on a busy Saturday night. We could barely move, but when we got into the ladies' locker room, we had some breathing space.

We got out and had about ten minutes to spare before race time. We looked around to find Linda and Laura, our other two teammates. They were nowhere to be found.

We walked outside in the pouring rain. Many of the runners were cutting through the local cemetery to get to the start line. I was going to follow but then Colleen said, "That's disrespectful." She was right. Colleen, Merrill, and I walked around the corner to get to the start line.

We tried to inch our way to the back of the start line. We wanted the runners trying to qualify for the Boston Marathon to go first.

At 8 a.m., we heard the horn, and runners were starting to take off.

Between the app, the Garmin and the Gymboss timer, which all had to be turned on, it was a little chaotic. Then, my phone wasn't working! I killed a lot of time toying with my gadgets.

Merrill, Colleen, and I started together. I was going to stay with them doing fifteen–thirty, but I needed to pick it up and go out a little harder because I wanted to PR this race. So, I left them. Colleen caught up to me doing fifteen–thirty and then noticed that Laura and Linda were in front of us. I ran over to them. Laura gave me a high five.

We stayed together for a little longer and then I started to run one minute and walk thirty seconds. I originally planned on a thirty-second run/thirty-second walk.

I left them and continued. The next few miles were uneventful. They seemed to pass quickly, and I was in my own head the entire time. The rain hit my body and I could feel a cool breeze, but I almost had an "out of body" experience. Even though I was completely drenched, I didn't feel the rain. It was a strange feeling.

At miles six and seven, we went through the grounds of a mansion and, as we were exiting the area, there were lawn signs with various military personnel who served our country. Some passed while others were deployed. All were from Long Island and, as I ran through this section, I became very emotional. Those men and women had dedicated their lives for us. I said a prayer for all of them.

At mile nine, as I was going downhill through an overpass, there was a huge puddle that was unavoidable. My feet were totally drenched! The water went all the way to my ankles. I cursed. I know, I know . . . I couldn't help it. I went nine miles avoiding puddles and this one got me.

I had four miles left. I kept telling myself, "I need to PR," but I couldn't gauge how fast I was going because my watch was unreadable due to the rain. I just wanted to step it up. My husband kept telling me I don't get out of my comfort zone. I was determined to prove him wrong.

Bystanders were on the streets cheering on the runners, even though it was one of the nastiest days of the year. I was totally amazed.

Mile ten, I thought, there was only another 5K left. I felt good. My knees hurt a little, but I kept moving forward. I changed my run–walk ratio to a fifteen-second run–fifteen-second walk and, oftentimes, I ended up doing one minute–fifteen seconds instead of fifteen–fifteen. I found though, that I was running slower than I had been. I typically run a nine-to-ten-minute mile pace and walk a twenty-minute mile, but now I was running an eleven-to-twelve-minute mile pace. My legs just didn't want to cooperate with my brain.

Mile twelve, I smiled at all the volunteers and police officers and said out loud, "One more mile, one more mile . . ."

At mile thirteen, I saw the start line but wasn't sure where the finishers chute was, so I asked a police officer. "You're right there," he told me.

I finally picked up the pace, when I heard the cheers from the crowd and heard Terry, the announcer, say, "Here's Hilary Topper, we were waiting for you. She's the owner of a public relations firm and a professional blogger." I was a little confused about his comment, "We were waiting for you," but I was grateful that he mentioned my PR firm and blog.

The volunteers gave me a heating blanket, a medal, and a small towel. I looked at my time and my heart raced. I PR'd this race by eight minutes! I was amazed. This was a hard one because the weather was so nasty, but I was excited that I finished strong.

Time: 2:50:00

Getting a PR was important to me because I wanted to prove to myself mostly that I could push harder. It felt so good to conquer this race in the rain with my teammates. But don't ask me to do it again! I'm just lucky my car didn't get stuck in the mud!

Lesson Learned

Giving back feels good. And, if it feels good, do it! When you give back, you feel like you have purpose. It also motivates you to keep on your path.

CHAPTER 22

Getting Out of My Comfort Zone

During that first year with the running group, I also trained and raced myself. If the training was light with the team, I would go the extra miles. As for my personal life, my husband and I sold our home of twenty-five years in Lido Beach and bought another one in Merrick, about twenty minutes away. My business stayed status quo. We moved into a larger office in Long Beach to spread out a little.

MEMORIAL DAY—BOLDERBOULDER

A memorable race I did during the year was the very old and famous BOLDERBoulder in Colorado. I was totally psyched to do it.

When I signed up, I didn't know what to expect. Everyone, including my coach, told me to beware of the altitude and stay hydrated. I used to ski in Colorado all the time, and I knew first-hand what altitude sickness was like—not fun.

I arrived in Denver a few days before the race and stayed with my cousin, Mindy. Then, the two of us headed up to Boulder.

The race was scheduled for Memorial Day morning. Fifty thousand people from around the world participated. My corral was up 8:15 a.m. The horn blew, and we were off. It seemed as though the entire town of

Boulder and surrounding areas came out for the race. There were more than 100,000 spectators. The crowds were cheering, and it was truly exciting.

On practically every corner, there were bands or even belly dancers entertaining us, crowds spraying water on us, and people throwing marshmallows at us! Many of the runners got off the route for a moment to slide down neighbor's Slip 'N Slides. There was even a Boulder resident offering their pool to take a quick dip before heading back on the racecourse. Everyone was there, including an Elvis impersonator singing all his "oldies but goodies." There were even a bunch of runners dressed as bananas running alongside me.

The hill entering Folsom Field, where the University of Colorado Boulder stadium was located, was tough!

Once we got passed that, we all ran a loop around the stadium. It felt as if we were in the Olympics. The stadium was packed with people watching and cheering. As we crossed the finish line, we were shuffled to an area where we collected our finisher water, soda, beer, and snack bags.

The race was complementary because of my two blogs—HilaryTopper.com and ATriathletesDiary.com. The organizers wanted me to share my experiences on the blogs. The coolest thing about this race was after I finished, I went on the press truck to follow the elite women runners.

These women were running fast! They ran a five-minute mile, and it was awesome to witness. Following the race, I had the opportunity to interview them, which I found so exciting!

It was an amazing way to spend Memorial Day, and it was probably the most fun I ever had at a race!

JUNE

At that point in my training, I was still uncertain about my swimming abilities. Every year since I started training for triathlons, the first open water swim felt scary. I never believed in myself, and I felt unsure about my abilities, and I was nervous that

- I would forget how to put on my wetsuit,
- I would forget how to swim,
- I would forget to spray my neck so that I didn't get chafed, or
- I would have a panic attack in the water.

This year, I faced those fears with my first open water swim of the season with the Total Masters Swimming group at Tobay Beach.

This season, one of the triathletes had put three buoys out so that we could all better track our swimming routes. One buoy was next to a tree that looked like a Bonsai, so we called it that. The middle buoy was about 100 yards or so from the beach, and the third buoy was by the marina. To swim between the farthest buoys was approximately 650 yards.

I thought the water would be cold since it was chilly in the Northeast at that time. As I entered the water, I literally tripped on something and fell in. But the water wasn't bad. It felt refreshing. It wasn't cold at all!

I started to swim and by the time I looked up, I was at the Bonsai tree. Wow, that felt good! The year before, I could barely get to the tree and during this swim, I was already there!

The longer I was out there, the more efficient I became. Even after swimming more than 2,500 yards, I wasn't tired. I wanted to keep going. I was in my happy place. I forgot how wonderful it felt to be in the open water.

When we ended, I just wanted to scream and shout and do a crazy dance on the beach to celebrate finally feeling relaxed in the water. It was a total breakthrough for me. I swam until the sun set. It was magnificent.

Instead of dancing and singing, I held myself back. The breakthrough that I had that night stayed with me for years to follow.

SEPTEMBER AND THE ROCK 'N' ROLL SAN JOSÉ EXPERIENCE

I never ran a Rock 'n' Roll (RNR) race but always wanted to. The RNR races are special. They focus on having music themes at every race. The reason why this one stood out so much was because I did it with my son. I was visiting him in college. He went to the University of California, Berkeley, and I noticed that the RNR had a San José run. San José was only an hour or so from Berkeley, so my son and I decided to do this one together.

At about 7:45 a.m. the next morning, Derek and I walked about two blocks to the start line and stood in our corral. I noticed that many of the tech companies, including Google, PayPal, and Strava, had teams on the course. I thought that was cool. You don't see that in New York!

When it was our turn, I turned on my timer, set it for thirty–thirty and turned on my Garmin to get started.

I didn't know if Derek would stay with me, but he wanted to. For a while, we played cat and mouse. We would run together then he would walk faster, then I would run to him, then we would walk, etc. Running with my son was an incredible experience. It made me so proud to run with him and spend quality time. I was also grateful that he enjoyed spending time with me!

The route also had lots of local cheerleaders. There was one family even giving out "free hugs."

For the first three miles we kept at a thirty-second run–thirty-second walk pace. It felt nice and easy. After that, I wanted to step it up a little to twenty-second run–twenty-second walk, then forty-second run–twenty-second walk, then sixty-second run–twenty-second walk. Derek kept up just fine. He liked the recovery walk incorporated into the runs.

We started to go faster the last mile. I felt amazing. He was hurting a bit but wanted to keep going strong. So, we picked up the pace and ran to the finish line. We crossed the finish line together. I was so proud of him for finishing the race and sharing the experience with me! And, we even had a nice negative split. When you run, you always try to aim for a negative split, meaning you are slower in the first half and faster in the second half of the run. It was a much more efficient way to run.

NOVEMBER

Miami Man Triathlon was on my bucket list for a long time. The international race was a half-mile swim, twenty-two-mile bike, and a 10K run. Since I went to Florida often to visit my dad, I thought I would sign up.

At 4 a.m., I got myself ready for the race.

I parked and the nerves kicked in, making me throw up. I know, too much information, but I couldn't stop. I was embarrassed. Some of the triathletes walking by were making comments. I ignored them. I got nervous at all triathlons. But this one I was especially nervous about because my dad, my brother, and his family would be there.

I pulled myself together, went over to transition and set up.

An announcement came on: "Wetsuits are not legal in this race. The water temperature is too warm." There was a collective sigh. Most triathletes don't like to swim without a wetsuit.

At 7:30 a.m., I headed over to the beach where the swim was starting. I noticed that people were practicing. I wondered if I would have issues with the swim with no wetsuit. I saw a few people wearing swim skins, a thinner, non-buoyant alternative to a wetsuit. I left mine back at the hotel. Oh no!

I got into the water and tested it. I focused on extending my arm into the water and then having high elbows under the water to pull my body along. I focused on the kick. I felt awesome. The water was crystal clear, and it was fresh water. Fresh water, what a treat! I assumed that because we were in Miami, it would be salt water, but this was in a lake within Miami.

I knew I would be fine once I was in.

Three, two, one . . . we were off. We ran into the water. As soon as I was knee deep, I started to swim. I could hear Bryan from Open Water Swim LI saying, "JUST GO . . ."

I swam around the lake. It was magnificent. Between the surroundings and the cool fresh water, I felt like I was in heaven. I saw the swim exit. I noticed people easily climbing out. I had a bit of a dizzy spell——stood up and shook it off.

I ran into transition, quickly put on my gear, and headed out with the bike.

I mounted and took off. The first five or so miles were a breeze. I was going at a nice pace of seventeen miles per hour. I was feeling happy. I love this sport.

There was a lot of traffic on the streets. The police watched and stopped the cars as the cyclists drove by but, at times, cyclists were going in and out of cars. It was very dangerous.

By mile six, I was head on into the wind. I kept pushing forward, but I was having issues. I was finding my seat uncomfortable, and my butt was burning. Also my gears kept getting stuck. I could barely keep a pace of ten miles per hour.

As I was pushing, a woman I had been talking with earlier caught up to me and was about to say something when suddenly, I saw another woman get very close to her. At one point, they were so close to each other, I didn't know what was going on. Were they doing that on purpose? And then, I saw the crash. She flew off the bike and went down. The other woman circled around to see if she was okay and I was in a situation that if I stopped, I would have crashed, too, so I had to keep going.

I felt so bad, and for the next few miles, my head was in a negative place. I couldn't wash away the image of the woman flying off the bike and, yet, she was coming to say something to me. What was she going to say?

Since there was nothing I could do at that point, I focused on trying to fight the wind. People passed me and I thought they were saying negative things to me. I wasn't sure what was happening. The heat was starting to get to me, too. I could feel the burning on my back. I was uncomfortable and starting to feel miserable.

Finally, I had the bike finish within my sights. I was glad I brought my bike computer to see the distance. It was shorter than I expected, but I couldn't even fathom the idea of doing that route again.

I dismounted and tried to run the bike into transition. I put on my sneakers and ran out for the run.

The start of the route was gorgeous. We ran around the lake we swam in, and then through some back trail areas until we reached the Miami zoo. Then we ran through the zoo and saw the elephants, rhinoceroses, and gazelle. That was cool but didn't last long because we were quickly out of the zoo and back in the outer areas.

There was ample water on the course. I needed it. We all needed it. The sun was blazing hot. I felt as if I were going to pass out. Every time I was just about to feel like I couldn't go on I saw a water station, dumped a cup of water on my head, and felt a little better to move forward.

I was not alone. I saw elite athletes walking. I saw so many people walking at one point I wondered if this was just a walk and not a race. I did fifteen-second run–thirty-second walk and then thirty-second run–fifteen-second walk. I tried to push but after that bike, I found it nearly impossible.

I thought I would see my family as I crossed the finish line, but I didn't. I heard the announcer say, "Here's Hilary Topper, chief curator of *A Triathlete's Diary*." I smiled. I finished the race, and I was still standing!

I was handed a gorgeous medal, a wet towel for my neck, and a can of Coke. I called my brother and he told me they were still in the zoo. I told them to enjoy and that I would meet them back at the hotel. To this day, my father doesn't forgive my brother for standing in the wrong place . . . haha. I'm still not sure why he didn't stand by the finish line!

After the race, the organizers had chicken and rice and pizza for all the athletes. I took a slice but couldn't eat it. As I sat at the table drinking my Coke, another triathlete told me that she'd been racing this race for eight years and that the conditions were most brutal this year.

I called Danielle and said, "Although the conditions were vicious, I'm glad I did it. I wanted to finish the triathlon season strong, and I felt like I did just that."

Lesson Learned

If someone is going to watch you in a triathlon, make sure that they meet you at the finish line.

2018

"When I find myself worried or deep in negative self-talk I have to actually go really, really basic and my quote to myself is literally just, "You can do this. Left. Right. Left, right."
–Gina Cornell, Six Ironman attempts, Wisconsin

CHAPTER 23

Losing My Best Friend

I was gearing up in January for a fantastic season. I scheduled the SHAPE Women's Half Marathon in April with my running team and then I was going to fly down to Saint Petersburg, Florida, to participate in St. Anthony's Triathlon for my birthday. It was a race I wanted to do for years. I joined Team in Training and raised $1,700 for the Leukemia and Lymphoma Society to race there. I even signed up for my second attempt at doing a Half Ironman in Augusta, Georgia.

However, everything came to a complete halt on April 9th when Lori, who I talked with hours before, was rushed to the hospital. She was in a coma. My sister had been complaining about headaches the week before, but no one thought anything of it, including her doctors. They thought it was just a migraine, nothing more.

Turned out Lori had had a massive stroke and aneurysm, which led to eighty percent coverage in her brain. When the doctors saw us at the hospital, they wanted us to make the decision whether she should have the surgery or not. If she didn't, she would die. If she did, there was a chance that she could recover. The doctors wanted to try to stop the bleeding in her head by inserting material into the aneurysm so blood could no longer flow through it.

When we couldn't decide, the doctors convinced us to have the brain surgery in hopes of a more promising outcome.

As you know, Lori and I celebrated our birthdays on the same day. When April 25th came around, her daughters decorated her room with the big 60 all around and we sang "happy birthday" to her. I was hoping for a steak and sushi dinner at Blackstone Steakhouse with Lori to celebrate our birthdays together, but instead her daughters and I sat and cried in palliative care. We knew the end was near and inevitable.

Nearly one month later after she entered the hospital, she died.

The races that I thought were important to me, weren't important any longer. The training that I enjoyed became a torture chamber for me. All I could see was my sister lying in a hospital bed with tubes coming out of her head, her belly, her arms, everywhere. It was so disturbing.

At the funeral, I read the following letter that I wrote to her:

Dear Lori,

It's your 60th birthday and it gives me an opportunity to reflect on all the things we shared and experienced through the last 56 years of my life.

For starters, I'm sorry I arrived on your birthday. I hope I didn't make too much of a mess at your 4-year-old party. Hopefully, mom went ahead with it, and you got to enjoy everything that you wanted.

Mom used to tell me I was your birthday gift. I'm not sure if I ever believed her but I think she tried to make you feel better that I was born on your birthday!

I always looked up to you. You were my role model. You introduced me to the good things in life, cigarettes, pot, alcohol, boys, and drugs. Haha . . . Do you remember when the boys used to climb up the back of the house and knock on my door. "Is your sister home?" they would ask.

I never said anything to Mom, but I begged for a curtain over the door after that!

After a breakup with your fiancé, I had the brilliant idea of telling Brian that I thought you and Gary should get together. It may have been a blessing and a sin because shortly thereafter, the two of you got married. You had an amazing dream wedding.

I remember when you were pregnant with Stefanie. OMG did you complain! And then, you had her early. I was there outside the door at Stony Brook Hospital as you screamed in pain. And then, everything got quiet. The next thing I knew, a beautiful baby girl was being taken down the hall. She was so small with the cutest little hat.

And I remember how she was in the NICU and we didn't know what was going to happen. You visited with her every day after she was born. Mom was there too. That was one of the hardest times in your life, but you were so strong and got through it.

Do you remember my wedding? Do you remember when you and Gary were both maid of honor and best man and when you left, you guys saw an accident and Gary destroyed your dress to help the car accident victim. I know how much you liked the dress . . . haha . . . Not!

Fast forward three years, and another cherub entered the world, this time it was Jessica. What an amazing baby Jessica was, and I was in love with both of my nieces. I felt like the luckiest person in the world!

After a bad divorce which left Brian and me stuck in the middle— between you and my brother-in-law . . . I often wondered if we made a mistake introducing you. It caused so much conflict between our families and at the same time our best friends were getting divorced. I felt like my world was shattered!

You got through it. We all got through it. I was so proud of you. You decided to go back to school and get your degree. I always knew you had it in you to be a nurse. You loved that. Dad always talked about when you dissected a pig or was it a cat? I don't remember. Whatever it was, it stunk up the whole house!

You raised those two amazing girls on your own and look at them now? They are incredible people. I know how proud you are of them both. And Finley, I know he is the love of your life.

You married Eric sometime after that and raised his two children. I thought it was the perfect family. You had two, he had two and you even talked about having another . . . But unfortunately, that didn't last.

In life, you must go through a series of tests before you find your true love, and I know you found that in John. He treated you with respect, dignity and was always there for you. He was completely different than the others. He was special, and he was your best friend.

I remember your 50th birthday going to the vineyards and getting totally drunk, singing songs, and having a total blast. And I remember when you surprised me for my 50th.

Then our world stopped when Mom died just a month or so later. It was horrible. It hit you so hard. It hit me so hard too, but we handled it differently.

But it wasn't all sad stuff, we shared some amazing times together like when we decided to get massages for our birthdays one time or when we just had a quiet meal with the boys or with each other. I loved celebrating our birthdays together! It meant the world to me.

It wasn't even a year ago when we flew down to Florida together to visit Dad. I was nervous that we wouldn't get along and would fight. But it really turned out great. We shared so many secrets, things I never knew about you. It was a total bonding experience.

Fast forward to three weeks ago, we had a conversation about Mom dying and how she died so young. "You know, it's not that far away. You ever think about that?" I said. "Yeah, that's why I want to live my life and travel and just enjoy everything with John," you told me.

"What do you want to do for your birthday?" I asked you. You said an experience. I said, "Let's go back to the vineyards." It was so stupid that we couldn't find a weekend until July or August! It was ridiculous!

You told me you wanted to go to Blackstone Steakhouse. I wanted to buy you a little something because our vineyard trip was far off. I wanted to get you something that was meaningful, so I bought you a locket. I cut out pictures of you and me and put them in the locket.

Then this happened. I am glad that you called me in the morning. And I'm glad that we said "I love you" as we always did every time we spoke. I wished I had spent more time on the phone with you that day. I felt rushed and it wasn't private speaking at work. But we said, "I love you."

Lori, I may have been mad at you for stupid things and I'm sure you were mad at me too. That's what happens with sisters. But I want you to know that I always loved you and always looked up to you. You were my sounding board, as I was yours.

You raised two amazing girls, had a wonderful job that I know you loved. You also had a guy who was there for you 100 percent of the time and a dog, Gino, who you were crazy about, although no one else was. You saw something in him that no one saw.

You did good. You had a good life.

You were an amazing sister who has helped me more than you can know. Thank you for always being there for me.

I really believed in my heart that we would grow old together and we would talk about the grandkids and great grandkids. I never would have thought this would have happened. Not to you!

I've learned my lesson here - never take for granted anything in your life—not your parents, not your siblings, not your spouse, not your friends, not even your children because you never know what will happen.

I will love you through eternity.

Love, Hilary

****

Believe it or not, a week after the funeral, my husband's family had scheduled a cruise for all of us to go on. It was planned two years before. I wasn't going to go. How can I enjoy something after my sister went through all of that? But, after some convincing from my family and friends, I went. Over the two-week cruise, I started to come to terms and deal with my grief.

A triathlete named Gina reached out to me before I left. She made triathlon kits and wanted to know if I could review for my blog. I agreed. On the ship, she told me a story about her friend who had suffered an aneurysm. Her friend was only thirty-five. Sadly, her friend passed away shortly after that and the two of us became instant friends, supporting each other through the aftermath of each other's tragedies.

I started reading posts on Facebook about people getting upset that they couldn't complete their training, or they feared their training, or they had a minor setback. I kept thinking, does any of this really matter?

I started rethinking my season after this happened. There were things in my life way more important than competing in a triathlon or even running a marathon. I competed for fun. I did it to challenge myself. I did it to get healthy. I did it because I loved it. But after what happened to Lori, I needed to rediscover my love for triathlon.

Lesson Learned

Appreciate the people who are important to you. Don't wait to say how you feel because if you wait, it may be too late.

CHAPTER 24

Races Where I Had to Dig Deep

After the 2016 NYTRI Expo, I decided to put together a triathlon team of people across the county and throughout the world. I named it, WeRTriathletes. The group included athletes from London, Paris, Madrid, and Berlin. We had members from as far away as Oregon, but most of the members were from the New York Metropolitan area. I also still had my run–walk group and I kept them separate.

JULY FIRE ISLAND SWIM

I hadn't raced since my sister passed. I couldn't get my head into the training. When I worked out, all I could think about was her lying there with tubes coming out of her head. Or the time when her boyfriend, two daughters, and I went into the operating room, looking like we were medical MDs.

When the doctors took out her breathing tube, they said she had one hour to live and, if she passed, they would donate her organs. If she didn't, she would go back up to palliative care. That one hour was the longest one hour in my life. We played music. We told her it was okay to go, but she hung on. She died almost two weeks after that with no food, just morphine, as she wished.

The experience was traumatic. It made me think about my own life. Will this happen to me at fifty-nine? The whole ordeal kept coming back in my head and I couldn't wash it away.

Although this was going through my head, I knew I needed to get back to reality. So, I signed up for this ocean swim, and when race day arrived, I drove to Bayshore Marina where I stood in line to catch the 9:15 a.m. ferry to Fire Island.

As I was standing there with dozens of swimmers, Coach Christine told us what to expect. We were body-marked and boarded the ferry. It took about twenty minutes or so and then we were there. I got off the boat and followed the swimmers down to the water.

When I got to the beach, I noticed that there was more than just a current, the water was stirring. At first, it didn't look bad but, as the morning got underway, the waves looked like a washing machine, and there were some big waves out in the middle of the ocean.

I walked over to the water and put my feet in. The water was freezing. I was told by the race director that it was sixty-four degrees Fahrenheit. I listened to the race briefing but anxiety started to set in. Will I be able to put my face in the water? Am I strong enough to fight the chop and the current?

Danielle told me to sight the beach and keep my head down. Can I do that?

There were many different divisions—400-meter swim, one-mile swim with wetsuit, one-mile swim without wetsuit, 5K swim with wetsuit, and 5K swim without wetsuit. The swimmers in the 5K wetsuit and non-wetsuit divisions went in the water first. (Many high school and college swimmers find that wetsuits are too restrictive, and some opt not to wear one.) Wetsuits do give you an advantage. Many people swim faster in a wetsuit, so race organizers judge swimmers in different categories depending on whether they are wearing a wetsuit.

Shawn, my friend who runs Total Master Swimming, was in the 5K no wetsuit division. I watched as he entered the water. Irene, a friend from Iron Fit Endurance, wore a wetsuit for the 5K swim. She was in a different division from Shawn.

As I stood and waited for my group to get in the water, I noticed that at least two or three people dropped out. The water was way too cold and choppy!

The wetsuits and non-wetsuits went together for the one-mile swim. I was in the wetsuit division. The horn went off. Some of us were reluctant to dive in. I was one of them. I needed to acclimate to the water temperature. Another swimmer was beside me. She said, "I'm getting out. You with me?"

"No, I'm going to go for it," I said, and I swam toward the turn buoy.

My face was burning from the water, but I forced myself to try to do this.

I saw Bryan at the start. He was on a jet ski and noticed panic on my face. "Hilary, just remember your training," he said.

I slowly started to get into a rhythm. Going to the first half-mile wasn't horrendous. It was rough, but the current and the wind took me. I passed one orange buoy, stopped, caught my breath, then went on to the next buoy.

The lifeguards in the water kept asking me if I was okay. I said I was and watched as more and more people were getting pulled from the water.

I finally made it to the yellow turnaround and started to head back. Every time I took a breath, water would get into my mouth. I remembered what Danielle said, "Sight on the shore and keep your head down." I tried, but it was hard. I was rocking and being tossed around like a rag doll. I could see the lifeguards in the water in my peripheral vision. Every time I picked my head out of the water to catch my breath; I was asked if I wanted to stop.

"I'm going to get this done," I said, "Whatever it takes. I am strong. I can do this." When you really want to do something and prove it to yourself and everyone else, the drive is a reality.

I made it to the next buoy after the turnaround. Okay, only a few more, I'm almost done. But I wasn't almost done. The second half took much longer than the first.

I tried to breathe out of my left side. I typically breathe out of my right side only. I was thrown around by the waves. I alternated and breathed as the waves were coming toward me.

I started to think about the first time I did a triathlon in Captiva where the water was very choppy, and I got through it. I loved it. Do I love this? Yes, I loved this. It was fun.

Bryan's jet ski came toward me as I stopped. "Am I the last one out here?" I asked him jokingly. (He's heard this from me a million times!)

"No, but if you were, what difference would it make? Just get it done. That will be an accomplishment!" he said.

I was about 200 meters back before the final turn buoys and I stopped. I needed to breathe. I never took my inhaler. My asthma was acting up and my breathing was heavy. I could feel myself wheezing. I'm not going to let this keep me back. I swam toward the yellow buoys. "How much longer?" I asked one of the lifeguards.

"Not much, do you want to DNF?" he asked.

"Absolutely not! I am going to keep going," I said.

I started having thoughts about my sister and my mother. They both were such strong women. The pain that they endured toward the end was in my head. Neither one of them wanted to die. They pushed and pushed until the end and that's what I was going to do. I didn't know if I would drown, but I was going to finish this race.

I finally got to the yellow buoys, and I thought it would be easy getting in, but it wasn't. I swam hard but felt like I wasn't going anywhere. Another lifeguard stopped me. "You, okay? Do you need help getting in?" he asked.

"No, I'm okay," I said.

I swam until a wave took me under and I was tumbling within it. I stayed calm. I wasn't going to freak out. I knew it would end soon. And, as it did, I picked myself up and there was a lifeguard beside me.

"Do you want me to run you in?" he said.

"Ha . . . no, I'm okay," I said. And I ran to the finish line.

As I exited onto the shore, I saw Shawn and he congratulated me. He told me he received a DNF because he was getting hyperthermia from not wearing a wetsuit.

I needed to walk around and met up with one of the referees from U.S. Masters Swimming. She was a volunteer.

"Wow, that was hard," I said.

"I know," she replied. "There were forty people rescued, more than a dozen who decided not to finish, and three people taken to the hospital. If you finished, you did good."

I felt good.

I felt proud of myself for doing something that so many people couldn't do. I dug deep, and I did it. I did it not only for myself but in memory of my beautiful sister and for life.

I went over to see how I ranked and noticed I was first in my age group. Wow, what an accomplishment.

At the awards ceremony, two older guys placed first and second in their age group, and one of them said, "I guess slow and steady wins the race."

That resonated with me. Slow and steady sometimes does win the race.

SEPTEMBER AND THE MIGHTY HAMPTONS TRI

You know Murphy's Law, "anything that can go wrong, will go wrong?" That is what happened to me at the Mighty Hamptons race.

The race itself is a class act. It takes place in the beautiful Sag Harbor area of the Hamptons. The swim is on a gorgeous beach. The bike portion takes you on a tour of amazing homes and farmland, and the run is simply magnificent. I could understand why Steve Tarpinian, master triathlete and the founder of EventPower LI, who tragically died in 2015, called this his favorite race.

Besides the beauty of this race, this race was difficult. Some years, it was easier than others, but this year, 2018, it had some of the toughest conditions.

At 4:45 a.m., I looked at my phone. My alarm never went off. I needed to be at the race site between 5:00 and 5:30. I jumped out of bed. I was staying at Forever Bungalows in Sag Harbor, a cute little bungalow colony for weekend renters. I was glad I was so close to the site. I put on my WeRTriathletes tri kit and started to apply the tattoos for the body marking.

I quickly noticed that my bike, helmet, and running belt said I was "399" but my tattoos said I was "398." So, I didn't apply them.

At 5:15 a.m., I arrived at the race site. It was less than ten minutes from where I was staying. I didn't sleep well. I wasn't nervous about the race, but I was still trying to come to terms with my sister's sudden passing a few months before. Different scenes popped in my head and replayed over and over, which prevented me from sleeping.

I went to the bike tent and asked them to pump up my tires. I was going to do it, but it was so dark, I couldn't see a thing.

After dropping off my bike, I went to get my timing chip. When I got there, I could see there was a problem. "We don't have a chip for you, but don't worry, we will take care of this. We're sorry. Don't let this spoil your race," the volunteer said to me. The timer came over and cleared up the mistake quickly and, after getting body marked, I went back to transition to set up.

There, I immediately saw my friend and running partner, Ray. This was his first triathlon, but I knew he would do great. Ray was tall, wore square glasses, and was an incredible athlete. At the time, I didn't know about his athletic abilities; I just knew he was a very nice guy and fun to train with.

His bike was next to mine. Funny coincidence! When Ray joined my running group a couple of months earlier, I had a gut feeling he would love triathlons. Who wouldn't love them?

He bought Matt Fitzgerald's book *80/20 Triathlon* after I reviewed it on my blog, and he used the training in there to get him to complete his first triathlon.

I set up and was ready. I put on my wetsuit and noticed that the water looked choppy.

I got in line for the swim and immediately saw coach, Danielle. She said that the water was choppy, "But you can definitely handle this. You swam in worse conditions this summer."

I was going to stay in the back because I didn't want to get kicked, but once I entered the water, I found myself in the front of the group. The gun went off and we were off. I swam nice and easy and had fun with it.

To me, the choppier the better. I'm not sure why I like it that way, but after swimming in Fire Island where it was also choppy, I started to really enjoy it. I had no issues with the swim. I swam out and back. A couple of times, people crossed over me but, like Shawn said, "Just stop and tread water. Let them pass and then you will pass them!"

The swim went quickly, and before I knew it, I was back at the transition area. All the bikes were in. I was in a good position, and I knew it. I got on my gear and ran out with my bike. At that very moment, I saw Coach Danielle. "You did great on the swim. I was spotting you and your stroke looked perfect," she said. I smiled. Now for the challenging part . . . the bike!

I hopped on and off I went. I was feeling strong in the beginning, and I knew what was ahead—a hilly ride. I was looking forward to it. I had done hills before in NYC, Milwaukee, Montauk, etc. But for some reason, between the cold weather, the wind, and the climbs, my chain dropped, and I fell off the bike.

"Bike down," some of the other triathletes yelled. A police officer came up to me.

I told him what had happened. As I was trying to fix the chain, Ray rode over. "Can I help?" he said. I was so grateful that he was there and was able to help me because the chain just wouldn't easily go on. The two of us were covered in bike grease, and I realized that it wasn't the chain but there was a piece that was bent and out of line on my derailer.

I told him I was good, and he waited for me to get back on the bike. I fell again. "Why don't you just walk it up and then ride?" he said.

He was right. I told him to go on his way. I didn't want him to have a bad race because of my mishaps!

I got back on the bike and fell again. The chain came off again. The police officer asked if he should get a patrol car to get me. "No, I'm going to get this done," I said. Now my bike computer was busted, my chain wasn't working right, but I was going to push on. "Hmm, I guess I'm now a true triathlete," I thought.

The rest of the ride wasn't easy for me because the chain wasn't right, and the gears weren't shifting. I was struggling. I kept thinking that I should end this. "A DNF isn't the worse thing in the world," I told myself. "It will make for a good story."

But every time I saw the police, I didn't stop. I forced myself to keep going. "Let me get through the bike and then I'll DNF," I thought.

I saw Danielle again on the road. She was running. "How's it going?" she asked.

"Not good," I told her. I went on to tell her I fell a couple of times because of a dropped chain.

"Okay, well you got this," she said. Then I rode away.

Finally, I got to the dismount.

As I was dismounting, another woman in my row said, "That's it for me. I'm done." Like me, she had just finished the bike. I thought about quitting too but something inside me said, "Just keep going." I'm constantly coaching myself through training and races. Every time I think "I can't," it motivates me to keep on going. I'll always feel the need to prove the doubters from my childhood wrong!

I put on my sneakers and headed out of transition. There was no one around me. I thought I was the last one on the course. I kept seeing tons of people heading in with everyone telling me, "You got this."

I started to get disheartened. I'm going to be dead f'ing last yet again. I started to think about the Wildwood Triathlon. But then I remembered what my sister once told me, *"It doesn't matter how you finish as long as you finish."*

Instead of being negative, I started to do the run–walk method first at fifteen-second run–thirty-second walk, then twenty-second run–thirty-second walk, then thirty-second run–fifteen-second walk, progressively running more each time.

I looked around at the beautiful course. I was happy. I was going to finish this. As I was running, I started to see lots of other people in front and behind me. "It's okay, I'm not going to be last." But it didn't matter if I was. All that mattered was that I finished.

I compared this race with the year I just had. I had so many obstacles thrown my way, and yet, I continued to move forward. I didn't want to, but I knew I had to, just like this race. I felt like if I made it to the finish line, I would cry.

As I was finishing the race, Laura was out at the finish line volunteering. She wanted to see Ray and me race since we all trained together.

Laura was one of my original members of my run–walk group. She was older than me and an amazing athlete. She won her age group most of the time! She was one of the nicest people I met in my triathlon journey, and I was so happy she was there.

Much to my amazement, I finished strong through the finisher's chute. Thankfully, I didn't take myself off the course.

Lesson Learned

Mechanical issues will happen. Currents and weather conditions also happen. You cannot control them. However, when you want to do something, you must mentally dig deep. Don't let those negative thoughts get in the way. Just focus on the moment and when you look back, you will see that you enjoyed it!

CHAPTER 25

50-Mile Relay With the Group

After leading two groups, WeRTriathletes, a group primarily for endurance athletes, and the WeRWalkRunLI, a walk–run group for Long Island runners, I decided to merge the groups and make one big group called WeREndurance Athletes. This was a triathlon/running team.

After the Mighty Hamptons Race, WeREndurance wanted a challenge and suggested doing a relay at the Ocean to Sound 50 Mile Relay. I thought this would be a good way to end the year, with my running family.

Long Island is simply beautiful. I love our sandy white beaches by the Atlantic Ocean, and I love the stunning marinas on the Long Island Sound. I feel so blessed to be living here.

Ray spent time figuring out everyone's times. He was a CFO at a local charity and was great at organizing things. "We may not make the cutoff," he told the group. But we decided we were going to do this for the experience. Each member of the relay team had a starting spot, and when a runner met their team members, they tagged them, and then the runner would continue until the end.

Text messages went back and forth. I loved all the excitement.

Since none of us had raced in the Ocean to Sound 50 Mile Relay before, we didn't know what to expect. The organizers weren't particularly helpful with the course directions. They handed us a map and told us to figure it out. I wished they had landmarks to make it easier for the runners. The day before the race, I walked my segment of the course because I wasn't quite sure where to go. I was starting the first leg.

When I got to the race start point at Field Two at Jones Beach, there must have been hundreds of people there. There was so much excitement from the other groups. You could also feel the nervous energy of the crowd.

At 7 a.m., I started out with a group of about thirty people. When the gun went off, I ran with the group. I couldn't even get close to anyone. They were so fast. My first mile was a ten-minute mile, and I didn't see anyone, except a for a woman in her seventies, once we got on the boardwalk. The woman was a little ahead of me and I was last. We ran on the Jones Beach boardwalk as the sun was rising. It was truly magnificent.

As soon as the boardwalk ended, I made a left out of Jones Beach. At that point, the woman was behind me. She caught up and said, "I don't like being last." She was an awesome runner.

I smiled and to be honest, I thought to myself, "If I can't outrun this seventy-year-old woman then I'm in big trouble."

The woman started to fade. I'm not sure if it was because of the heat or that she ran Cow Harbor the day before, which is what she shared with me as we were running. The Great Cow Harbor is one of the hardest races on Long Island, with steep climbs. Whatever the case, I didn't see her after the first twenty minutes or so into the run. I ran past her and then, I was alone.

I saw her support crew out on the Wantagh Parkway. I wished I had a support crew because I needed to pour water over my head! It was that hot.

I ran along the path from Jones Beach to Cedar Creek Park and loved every minute of it. As soon as I entered the park, Laura greeted me and gave me a high five and took off! She ran her six miles to Massapequa Preserve. Meanwhile, Dawn, one of my runners who became a dear friend, and her daughter met me at the park and drove me back to my car in Jones Beach. Dawn was one of the most positive people I met through training and always had a smile on her face.

When Laura got to Massapequa, she tagged another member who took off, and that's how it went for the 50 miles. We ended up doing it in under nine hours.

The course had lots of steep climbs and descents. The heat made it feel even harder.

As the last runner from our group was coming in, I noticed the volunteers taking down all the cones. I asked them to stay but they wouldn't. "We've been here all day and it's now time to party," the volunteer told me. That frustrated me.

I mean, I totally get it, but it still upset me. Our last runner was upset. She even had a police escort but turned them away. I asked them to watch her as she crossed Northern Boulevard and, happily, they did.

She had a half mile to go and a few of us went to the finish line. The guys were taking everything down. The announcer was starting to put away all his equipment too. I asked them all if they could wait five minutes until our teammate came in.

"It would mean so much to me," I begged. Thankfully, they didn't break down everything and Terry, the announcer for most of the races on Long Island, announced our group as she came in. We were all so excited. I'm grateful to those volunteers and to Terry for holding out a few minutes while we finished the race.

I'm not quite sure what the big deal with the party was. By the time we got there at 4:45 p.m., it was practically over. There were a few people dancing and a couple of cans of beer left. They still had some hamburgers and hot dogs. I didn't want to eat. I decided to talk with my team for a bit and then head home.

Lesson Learned

If you can find a team to be a part of, do it. Like-minded people will make your sport fun and will make the trainings enjoyable. The people in WeREndurance are some of my closest friends and I am truly blessed. To me, competing in triathlons and running events is so much more fun when on a team because of the camaraderie. I wouldn't have it any other way, and I hope that if you start your journey, you can find a team that will support you as well.

CHAPTER 26

Saint Croix's Beauty and the Beast Race

DECEMBER

Even though this was one of the hardest years for me, it ended with a bang and an amazing opportunity that I truly needed.

I received an email from a public relations firm asking if I would cover the Beauty & the Beast Triathlon in Saint Croix. They told me they would pick up my expenses if I competed and wrote about it.

I was in!

The Beauty & the Beast Triathlon is known to be one of the toughest triathlons out there because of its steep inclines. The Saint Croix Beauty & the Beast Triathlon had several different races: a 70.3, sprint, relays, and an Aquathon (also called an Aqua Run, which is a swim and a run). There were 170 participants, and the race was well-organized and well-orchestrated.

I participated in the Aqua Run. Originally, I was going to rent a bike and do a sprint triathlon, but those hills were mean. There was no way I wanted to attempt it. I even got to see the "Beast," and that looked like a crazy hill! I didn't train for hills and was just doing this race for the experience and to write about it.

We had to swim to another island to start the race. It was far, and I was thinking that by swimming this extra yardage it would make me tired for the race, but I was fine. As I swam to the island, I saw some beautiful turtles and other ocean wildlife. I was beaming!

The race took off, and I had a wonderful swim in the warm water. I swam past a pirate ship and exited to transition. From there, I went on the run.

The run was tough. It was hilly and hot. The volunteers gave out sponges and ice to the participants. That really helped!

When I finished the race, I was greeted by clowns and so many of the islanders. This may have been my favorite race so far!

A fantastic trip to Saint Croix and experiencing an Aqua Run ended 2018. As I flew home from the trip, I was excited about 2019 and what it had in store for me. I will never understand what happened to Lori, but I knew I had to live with it. All I wanted was for her to call me one more time and let me know she was okay. But you know, I sensed it. I felt her presence, and all I felt was pure love. She was with my mother and they were both at peace.

Lesson Learned

Unfortunately, losing people you love is something we endure in life. In between those tragic moments, life can be beautiful. It's up to you to choose between uplifting moments and tragic events. Go through life with a smile on your face, focus on those amazing times. Stay with people who make you feel good about yourself!

2019

CHAPTER 27

Trying to Pick Up the Pieces

2018 was mentally rough. I spent the year trying to pick up the pieces. I wanted to get back to running races with my running club and competing in triathlons.

Since my mother passed in 2012, I would visit my dad every couple of months. I needed to make sure he was okay even after he found a girlfriend, who in my opinion took advantage of his good nature. But he was in love, and I didn't say anything. I was happy that he was happy; no one should be alone. He took care of my mother for so many years. She was his life. When she was gone, he was lost. So, by finding Harriet, his new girlfriend, he was happy again. She was disabled, and my dad helped her with everyday tasks. She, in return, helped my dad with his dementia. It worked well for the two of them until she started to show signs of dementia, too.

At the end of 2018, my business moved to a smaller office in Long Beach and, again, I had staffing problems. I had a long heart-to-heart with Lisa, and we decided instead of hiring full time staff, we would farm out work to a group of trusted freelancers. Staffing issues really brought me down, demotivated me, and hurt the business.

Now I was at a crossroad once again between trying to get my business back, taking care of my dad, and making sure I continued my responsibilities at home.

In February, I headed back down to Florida with my kids to see my dad. I was preparing for two major events. I needed to get the miles in.

****

My kids and I were staying at the Hampton Inn on Commercial Boulevard near the Florida Turnpike, about a twenty-minute drive from my dad's place in Kings Point, Tamarac.

"Why don't you run from the hotel to Poppy's house?" my daughter said. My son looked up the distance. It was a little more than eight miles away.

"You can do it, Mom," he said.

The next day when we were in town, I scoped out the path. If I went straight on Commercial Boulevard to Hiatus and then made a right turn toward my dad's place, I could get this done. But was Commercial Boulevard accessible for runners?

I went to bed early the night before the run. I was nervous. Can I do this? "Yes, you can do this." I told myself. "You've done eight miles a ton of times. It's just another time . . ."

My back was hurting me all week. I was tired. I didn't feel like getting it done. I knew my running club had already run the eight miles in the freezing cold weather in New York. This was a perfect opportunity to run eight miles in beautiful weather. I think my biggest fear was that I never ran this route before, and I was afraid I would get lost. I hate running or riding in places I don't know because of that fear.

I got up at a reasonable time, went downstairs to the lobby, and tried to eat something. I drank a cup of coffee. My stomach was bothering me, but I thought it was my nerves. It probably was my nerves.

I went to the front desk and asked about the overpass over the highway. "Do you know if there is a sidewalk over the highway?" I asked.

"You know, I've never seen anyone walk over the highway," the front desk manager said to me. "As a matter of fact, I never see anyone walking on Commercial. Why don't you run around the Executive Airport, that's not far from here."

"Thanks. I think I'll try to figure it out," I told her and walked out the door.

I left the hotel and walked toward the highway. I passed a fire house and noticed a bridge that went over the highway. I was in luck.

I walked over to and up the bridge. This was my warm-up. As I looked down, all I could see were large trucks going eighty miles per hour. I decided to look away.

When I got to the end of the bridge, I had to cross the entry onto the highway. I was nervous because the cars were coming onto the highway fast, and I didn't want to get hit. I waited. When there was an opening, I ran across. Now, I was on the wrong side of the street.

I kept going. When suddenly I hit another roadblock, a golf course. There was no longer a sidewalk. I ran on the grass, but it was uneven, and I didn't want to run in the bike lane because Commercial Boulevard had four lanes in both directions, and the cars were speeding by.

There was a man in a car that pulled up on the golf course. I asked him where the sidewalk was. He told me to cross the street and get to the other side. But the cars were coming . . . would they stop? Would there be a break? I waited. There was a break, and I ran across the eight lanes. I was amazed. It was as if an angel was looking over me . . .

I ran past the Bedding Barn, and I got a call from my son, "You okay? Where are you?"

"I'm only about three miles in, five to go," I told him.

"Okay, I'll leave in an hour or so," he said. My son was meeting me at my dad's house with my change of clothes and accessories for the day.

There were lots of little strip malls on Commercial Boulevard, and I found that every time I tried to run a bit, there was another obstacle to face. There were lots of major roads where I had to stop and wait for the light to change while strangers would pass by me. It reminded me of life and how many curve balls we all face as we go through our lives. It even reminded me of my business. I had so many ups and downs through the years. I wish it were a steady up, but I know in my heart that the business is cyclical and the economy factors in.

I continued down to Hiatus Blvd. It took nearly six miles to get there and as soon as I did, I stopped at a gas station, got some water, poured some over my head to cool myself off and kept on going. I'm close. Two miles to go.

I ran down Hiatus Blvd. It was a long road past many commercial buildings and a big-box furniture store. There were gardeners there cutting the trees and the grass. I ran past them, holding my nose because the smell of fresh cut grass bothered me.

At the end of Hiatus, I went a couple more blocks and ran to 80th Street. I knew I was in the home stretch now. Derek called again. "I'm on my way," he said.

Soon after, I saw him as I was turning into Exeter/Granville in Kings Point. He was driving alongside me. "You got this, Mom. It's the home stretch."

He continued to drive to my dad's apartment, and I ran. I felt good, strong, and I wasn't tired.

I finally made it to my dad's apartment, after running–walking 8.1 miles with a negative split. It made me feel so happy that I forced myself to do it, and that I got it done.

When I came home a couple of weeks later . . .

I stubbed and broke my toe. When I went to the urgent care doctor, she told me to stay off it for six weeks. "No activity. No swimming. No cycling. And no running!" she told me.

Depression set in immediately following the visit. What about all the races I have lined up? Within the next six weeks, I had:

- Mardi Gras Race—7.1 miles in Bayshore
- Disney Princess—13.1 miles in Disney (I even bought an outfit!)
- NYC Half—13.1 miles in Brooklyn and Manhattan (I haven't done this race in years and was hoping for a PR! Waa . . .)

Then I was supposed to go skiing in Utah for a week. How was I going to do that if I wasn't in shape?

Six weeks was a long time to be inactive. I'd lose my fitness. I wouldn't be able to do St. Anthony's Triathlon because I wasn't training. What was I going to do?

Then, I stopped and thought about friends who were injured, and they got through it. I'll get through it, too.

I guess the point I'm making here is, stuff happens. And, there's nothing that we can do about it. All we can do is adapt to the situation and move forward.

A couple of weeks after I broke my toe, I realized that I could still cycle and swim. If I don't push on my toes and push through with my heels, I could ride and ride efficiently. And while swimming, the key was not to push against the pool wall with my bad foot. Thankfully, it all clicked, and at least I was able to work on those two disciplines for the first few weeks.

As I pushed through the pain, I just kept thinking, "It could have been worse." Maybe now, I was finally starting to see what people were saying to me during Hurricane Sandy.

Lesson Learned

If you're injured, remember, it's just a minor setback. Try to find something that you can do to stay active. You will come back even stronger than before!

CHAPTER 28

Being a Bystander

Since I already had my airline tickets, I decided to go with my two running friends, Didi and Colleen, to the Disney Princess Half Marathon Weekend.

The day of the event, my friends left the hotel at 2:30 a.m. to catch the bus to take them to the park. I left the hotel at 4 a.m. and didn't get on a bus until after 5 a.m. By the time I reached the park, my toe was bothering me. So, I hobbled to the Race Retreat area. We had purchased VIP tickets for before and after the race. Didi thought it would make the race more enjoyable.

To me, sitting on the sidelines meant I had the opportunity to cheer people on and experience the other side of racing.

For example, as I was waiting for my WeREndurance friends to come in, a young woman who had been paralyzed from an autoimmune disorder and had been struggling to get her life back, got out of her wheelchair and walked the last tenth of a mile of the half marathon. I watched this and chanted with the crowd. It was quite emotional.

I also felt like I was going to cry as I saw some of the runners struggle. And I did cry when my runners came in. I was choked up. One even ended up with a PR by eight minutes!

Sometimes things happen, and when they do, you just must take the bull by the horn, get out there, and be selfless while others achieve their dreams! It really does feel good to support fellow endurance athletes.

Lesson Learned

If you're injured or for some reason can't do a race with a friend or training partner, consider watching or volunteering. You will be surprised at how exciting the races are, and it will make you even more motivated to come back stronger.

CHAPTER 29

Finally Made It to St. Anthony's Triathlon

I finally made it to St. Anthony's Triathlon, but I was still going through a lot of emotions over my sister. I really was having a hard time dealing with everything. Mindy suggested that she go with me to the race and cheer me on. "And anyway, Hilary, I don't want you to be alone on your first birthday without Lori," she said.

Mindy and I grew up together. She spent most summers with my family, and we did everything together. We stayed close for many years and then, when we were teenagers, we lost touch for a while. When she moved to Denver, we rekindled our relationship. I always considered Mindy my middle sister. She had a lot of similarities to Lori, but she also was a lot like me.

Mindy was slim, had short blonde hair and beautiful green eyes. She loved clothes and shoes just as much as I did.

After arriving in Tampa and renting a car, Mindy and I checked into the Vinoy Renaissance Hotel, steps away from transition. After that, we walked around the transition site and the expo. On our way to the expo, we saw TriBike Transport, and I retrieved my gear bag.

The next day, I got my bike from TriBike Transport, and they filled up my tires and put on my pedals. I rode it, like my coach instructed, to make sure all the gears were working properly. It felt good to ride.

As I racked the bike, I went through the race in my head. I looked around and envisioned myself swimming in, riding out and running out. I stood in the middle of transition just looking at the run in/bike out spots.

I was one of the last ones to leave transition and didn't have time to make one last pit stop. As I was leaving, I asked a volunteer where the closest porta-potty was. She told me to use the volunteer one. "It's much cleaner," she said.

Boy, was she wrong! It was horrible. Plus, there was no toilet paper! As I left the hotel, I took a roll of toilet paper with me. But don't you know, I left it in the transition bag and was unable to retrieve it! "This isn't starting well," I thought.

I walked over to the swim start. "Maybe I can go in the water and clean up," I thought. No such luck! The water was low tide. The only way to get deep into it would be to stand alongside the competitors who were racing. I stood in the shallow water feeling very self-conscious. I brushed it off. "Stay in the moment," I heard my coach saying to me.

I lined up with the green caps. As I stood there waiting to enter the water, I heard, "Hilary!" I look up, and there was Mindy standing, cheering. I smiled. It felt so good to see her there!

The fifty to fifty-nine-year-old age group entered the water. We stood. The water was cold. It didn't look rough, but I did feel a bit of a current. I looked around. Everyone was shivering. There were some people without wetsuits, but most wore them. People were commenting that they didn't feel good in the water and that I should go in front of them. I kept in the zone just like my coach said.

The gun went off, and I began to swim, nice and easy. The water looked flat. I looked over and saw a woman doing the backstroke. I saw another one doing a breaststroke. Arms and legs were flailing all over the place. I kept in the moment. "Nice and easy," I thought. There's a long way to go.

Soon, I was at the first turn and went deeper into the open water. As I did that, the sixty-year-old men who were behind the women, came upon us. They were pushing and kicking. One guy tried to push me down to swim over me. I wanted no part of that! Swim faster, I thought, I need to get away from all those people and get into my own groove, and that's exactly what I did.

However, the water was rough, very rough. I smiled to myself. "The choppier the better!"

The swim course was nicely marked. There were many red buoys, which were for direction and yellow buoys, which were for turning. I felt as if I was going straight, which for me, was a huge accomplishment.

The course was along the beach and then went out and made a big box. It looked sort of like the "big dipper," someone told me. It was true.

"I got this," I thought, and I swam to the beach. As I approached the steps, two men pulled me out of the water. I stood there for a moment feeling dizzy and disoriented. Mindy screamed my name. I smiled again and ran into transition.

As I entered transition, I found my spot, sat down, and tried to pull off my wetsuit, but it wouldn't come off. I had never had this problem before! I had to struggle to get my legs out. Five minutes later, which is a rather long transition, I had my helmet on, unracked my bike, and was on my way.

I got on my bike and took off. Staying in the moment, I couldn't believe how pleasant the ride was. It was a tour of Saint Petersburg!

Now I could see why they say St. Anthony's Triathlon is flat and fast!

We rode past the Salvador Dali Museum and up and down the streets. The bike route was marked beautifully. This was one of the best-marked courses I had been on! So many times, I got on the bike, and I wasn't sure where to go. "Should I go left, or right?" I would often yell out to a volunteer. But, this time, I felt 100 percent comfortable. There were so many markers both on the ground and off the ground. There were cones that mapped out the direction along with great big signage!

One thing that I will say about the course was that there are a ton of sharp technical turns. There were several U-turns as well. I found myself slowing down for these turns, then finding it hard to get back up to speed. There was also a lot of wind, which made it harder to ride.

At times, we were on some very bumpy roads. At one point, I yelled to a volunteer, "Why are these roads so bumpy?"

He said, "Because the residents want it that way."

I was happy to get back on a smooth road. The bumpy roads were making me feel nauseous! I couldn't ride over them fast. The faster I went, the rougher it felt. I was thinking about some of the people who passed me. "How are they doing this?"

At mile ten, there was a bottle exchange. I didn't want to try to reach out and get water. So, I said, "Thank you" and rode on. About forty-five minutes into the ride, I ate a gel. In a conversation I had the night before with my coach, she instructed me to eat every forty-five minutes and constantly drink on the bike.

The ride back to transition had at least a block or two of brick road. It was very rough, and I slowed down into transition.

By the time I reached T2, I had to go to the bathroom. I couldn't run six miles without going. So, I made a pitstop into another one of those horrible porta-potties. At least this time, there was toilet paper.

I walked back to my spot, changed my shoes, and took off. The run was going to be the challenge of the day!

We ran out along the water and then into a gorgeous Saint Petersburg neighborhood. The homes were magnificent.

What I loved about the run was that people from the neighborhood came out and set up stands where they offered water, oranges, and shots of beer. I felt as if I were running BOLDERBoulder again! There was so much community outpouring of love. You could just feel it.

Some of the residents even had hoses going so competitors could cool off. The St. Anthony's Triathlon volunteers offered water, Gatorade,

Gu, and ice cubes. At every water stop, and there were a lot, at least one every half mile or so, I dumped water on my head to cool down. It was hot. The weather was ninety degrees at the time of the run.

The only problem was my Achilles. After breaking my toe in January, I ran the Riverhead Rocks race and pulled a muscle in the trails. Every time I ran after that, I would get severe pain in my ankle. I tried everything to make it feel better for the race, including not running for at least two weeks.

A couple of weeks before the race, I said to my coach, "I don't know if I can run again. Let alone six miles. It's been so long!"

She said, "If you feel better, you can easily run six miles."

With every step I took, I could feel the back of my ankle pulling. I kept thinking of Jeff Galloway and what he said to me about the Achilles. "You can run on it, but make sure to ice it two times a day!"

I needed to get through this race. I wasn't going to give up. Mindy was there to see me finish, although she said many times, "If something doesn't feel right, don't do it." I just wanted to show her I could do it. I wanted to make her proud of her "little sister." Although I used to beg Lori to see my race, she never wanted to. So, she never did. That disappointed me.

After passing the three-mile mark, we headed back to transition. A neighbor gave me an orange, which gave me a boost. I ate my gel and felt good. The only thing bothering me was my ankle and heel.

Although I tried ten–twenty, I tended to walk more then run. It was hot and I was hurting. I allowed myself to just finish. My goal was to finish and have a smile on my face.

I kept hearing my coach say, "Stay in the moment." I did. Taking in everything, I let myself enjoy the scenery.

When I got about fifty yards from the finish line, I sprinted. I didn't care about the pain, I wanted to cross the finish line with my signature pose. Mindy was cheering. I crossed the finish line and did what I set out to do. I was happy!

Lesson Learned

Although you may have missed a race one year, that doesn't mean that you will never get the opportunity to do the race. Lori would always tell me, "If it's meant to be, it is meant to be."

CHAPTER 30

Life-Changing Experiences

MAY

I continued to run with my running group. They were a big help to getting me through the trauma that I had experienced the year before. Everyone in the group had their own issues, and many had dealt with the death of a sibling, a loved one, and/or a child. We were supporting each other.

Every week, we would run between five to fourteen miles, depending on our goal. Some of the group wanted to focus on running a marathon, while others focused on running a 50K ultra-marathon, which is a little more than thirty-one miles.

I started to think about triathlons and thought maybe this sport wasn't for me. What am I doing? I have no goals, no motivation, and no drive. I told Danielle that I wanted to take a break. I was having such a hard time with everything. I kept focusing on my loss and not on what I had.

I still spent the summer swimming in the open water. I started training with Ray. He was a fantastic swimmer, and I could barely keep up with him.

Having someone to share something that I loved made me happy. He was a low-key kind of person, and we both focused on training. There was no drama. It was all about the training and getting it done.

When I swam in the water, I realized that being in the open water was my happy place. All the craziness in my head would disappear or sometimes reappear when I went swimming, but when it reappeared, I was able to work things out in the water.

TRAINING AT HOFSTRA

I constantly felt that throughout this journey, I struggled with weight loss. During my training for the New York City Marathon in 2016, I gained twenty pounds. I don't know if it was from the hydration I was drinking or what, but I gained weight from training.

I tried so many different plans like Weight Watchers, Jenny Craig, Optiva, and Atkins nothing worked. Then, I tried MetPro, and that's when I lost a good fifteen pounds.

So, on this day, I didn't realize that some of my XL bathing suits were a little too big. Hence, an embarrassing thing happened at the pool.

I threw a bathing suit in my gym bag, and I remembered to bring a towel to the pool. There were days that I would run out and forget the towel. And on those days, I would shake off really well before putting on my clothes. It was not comfortable at all!

I arrived at Hofstra Swim Center, went to the locker, and put on my bathing suit. It felt a little loose, but I didn't have another suit with me, so I kept it on.

After picking out a lane, I put all my swim "toys," which included my fins, pull buoy, paddles, and kickboard, at the edge of the pool. I put in my ear plugs, put on my bathing cap, goggles, and nose plugs, and sat there for a few moments, as I always do. You'd think after all these years of swimming, I would be accustomed to the water and yet, once I jump in, it was always a shock to my body.

I took the plunge and swam across the pool. It was amazing to me how easy it was to swim twenty-five yards at this point. I remember when I couldn't get across the pool.

Suddenly, I got the feeling that people were noticing me. Was I swimming particularly well today? Were people thinking that I was an efficient swimmer? I looked around. I wondered what they were thinking.

After about 500 to 1,000 yards, I noticed that my top half seemed like there was more water than usual. I almost felt as if I were skinny dipping and yet, I wasn't.

Or was I?

I stopped when I got back to the edge of the pool and look down. "OMG," I said to myself, "I am skinny dipping!" At that point, I noticed that my breasts were completely out of the bathing suit, and the bathing suit had drooped down.

Losing weight has its advantages and disadvantages. Now I know why so many people were looking at me!

TRAINING RUN AT NORMAN LEVY PARK

The running group went on a training run to Norman Levy Park in Merrick. The park is built on a garbage dump. They keep goats there and have turned it into an oasis of open space.

I got there late and parked my car. As I exited the car, Bill, one of the members of my group was looking at my license plate and said, "What does HJMT stand for?"

I told him, "Hilary Jan Mass Topper." He looked perplexed.

Bill was in his sixties and an amazing runner who has done several marathons. He loved to tell stories and kept the group on our toes with his detailed accounts of events from his past. I'll tell you, I never laughed so hard with this group. I loved these people.

Later that night, Bill sent me an email. "Hilary, do you know a Phyllis Mass or a Lori Mass?"

I wrote him back, "Yes, that is my mother and sister."

"What a small world," he wrote. "I met them at Camp Wildwood. Your mother worked at the candy shop and your sister was a waitress at the camp."

"That is so funny," I wrote back. "I can't believe you knew them."

On subsequent runs, I heard all the stories about my mother saving Hot Chili Peppers candy for him because that was his favorite and other stories about the camp. It was incredible to hear such awesome stories about both my mother and my sister from a different perspective. Such a small world!

Lesson Learned

If you lose weight, buy the right sized bathing suit!

CHAPTER 31

Turning Point in My Racing

I ran the New York Road Runners Mini 10K Event in Central Park three times—once in 2015, 2017, and in 2019. This was one of my favorite races, and that's probably because I ran it with my daughter. In 2019, I ran it with my daughter, her friend, Kendra, and some of the women in my running group.

Once the Mini 10K got started, we ran uptown on Central Park West before we headed into the park.

There was a big downhill in the park, but I knew what was coming. I tried to get in the speed on the downhill because once we got to Harlem Hill, I knew I would slow down. Funny, this time and at the Global Running Day event, I thought to myself Harlem Hill isn't as bad as I remembered. I wonder if I'm getting stronger.

The volunteers were encouraging. Spectators were cheering. Everyone was so supportive.

At this point, I was at mile four. I kept thinking, "Just two more miles to go . . ." I didn't feel bad, my Achilles bothered me as usual, but my hip was okay. I was pleasantly surprised because I rode my bike the day before the New York Road Runners Mini 10K, and my hip was killing me! Almost two miles to go . . .

I ran a slow fourth mile and then decided I needed to pick up the pace. I needed to move up to a faster corral. New York Road Runners always puts me in the last one! The heat was beating on my head. I couldn't wait to get to the water stop to pour water over it.

Mile five felt easy. I started to notice the pain in my Achilles less and just have fun with the race. There were times when I was running, and I felt like I was flying. Between the heat and running, maybe I was a little delusional? My music was playing, and I was in my zone. One mile to go. "I need to make this a good one," I thought.

I finished the race by hearing my daughter call out my name. That made me smile. I ran through the chute, felt the energy from the crowd, and my daughter's boyfriend, Dan, told me that I beat my race time from the prior years. "You killed it," he said.

Total time: 1:15:00

I was so excited that I had a PR. The hills didn't feel so hard, and the race wasn't as difficult as it was in the past. I was getting stronger and fitter, and I felt good about it.

When we each finished the Mini 10K, we were given a beautiful medal, a pink bagel, and a flower. I couldn't stop smiling.

AUGUST

The Long Beach Lifeguard Memorial Swim had been around for years. And I remember thinking it was only for lifeguards. So, when I found out this year it was open to all swimmers, I thought, "Sure, why not?"

I decided to swim the half mile. They had a one-mile option as well. The "little" half mile was more like 1,200 yards, according to my Garmin. Wetsuits were not allowed during the race. However, if you wanted to wear one, you could, but you weren't eligible for an award, and you got a five-minute penalty.

I didn't care. I wasn't looking to place. I was there to swim in the ocean and have a great experience. And that's just what happened.

We had to walk half a mile on the beach to get to the start. There were buses for the one-miler swimmers. But many of the one-milers walked.

My legs were burning as I plowed through the sand. I tried to go over to the harder sand to walk because I was finding it impossible to walk on the soft sand. As I was walking, I saw Becky. She was with a group of her new triathlon friends. We said hello, but it was only cordial. Ever since we started triathlons, we started to move away from each other. It made me sad, but that's what happens. People come and go in your life.

There were a handful of people at the start of the half-mile race. The race director took down my number to tack on the additional five minutes. So, going into the race, I wasn't thinking it was a race. I was thinking I'm going to go for a pleasant swim with other swimmers.

At 9:05 a.m., the race director blew the horn and twenty or so of us jumped into the water and swam to the buoy. The water was choppy but not as bad as it had been. We were swimming with the current.

As we swam, I felt as if I were on a waterbed going up and going down. I loved every moment of it! I was in my happy place, and I didn't want it to end. There was no one around me, and I felt at total peace and harmony with my body and with the ocean.

Growing up in Long Beach, one time I went to the beach with a ring my grandmother bought me. My mother told me not to wear it. I didn't listen. Of course, the ring got lost in the ocean. When I got home and told my mother, I was severely reprimanded and told that I had to get myself a job so that I can replace the ring.

"Your grandmother will never forgive you," my mother told me. And that's exactly what I did. I bought a new ring and replaced the one my grandmother had bought me. I never did tell my grandmother and had this guilt with me for many years to follow.

As I was swimming in the Long Beach Lifeguard Memorial Swim, deep in the ocean, I let it all go—my mother, my grandmother, the ring, and my fear.

My thoughts focused on the finish line, but I didn't want the finish to come . . . I was loving this swim.

At the last buoy, I turned and, suddenly, there were four or five swimmers around me. Now it was race time. Once I was in the water, there was no one around me and I felt like it was just a wonderful swim. I didn't understand where these people came from but as I started to pass them, they kicked it up a notch. I guess I should have too, but I was enjoying myself so much!

Total time: twenty minutes

P.S. I won second place in my division even with the penalty! Woo-hoo!

SEPTEMBER

I had so much fun at the Long Beach swim, that I decided to sign up for the Aqua Run at Tobay Beach in Oyster Bay.

When I got to Tobay Beach, I was one of the first ones to arrive. I grabbed my number and headed over to transition to set up. I was stationed next to a woman from the Brooklyn Triathlon Club. We chatted for a while, and then she went to stretch out and do some yoga before the event started.

I saw Monica from WeREndurance. We talked for a while, then I put on my wetsuit and headed into the water for a practice swim.

The water was freezing. I was glad I had my sleeveless wetsuit but secretly wished I had brought my long-sleeve wetsuit. I was talking with some people in the water. There was one woman from the Merrick Bicycles Triathlon Team who wasn't wearing a wetsuit. I asked her if she was cold and she said, "No." I was freezing. Putting my face in the water was difficult, and I was glad to do the practice swim before the event to get acclimated.

We were all called out of the water and waited for the start horn.

Before I knew it, I heard the horn and was running into the water with high knees.

Just as I was thinking, "I'm doing a great job at this," I tripped and fell into the water. Monica was behind me.

"Are you okay?" she asked.

I smiled, although I felt a little embarrassed. As we got into the deeper water, I swam, and I kept swimming until the end. It was a short half-mile swim. The buoys were well-marked and there was a ton of support on the course.

As I was swimming, several of the men in the forty-plus group caught up and passed me. It seemed as if there weren't any orange caps around me. I thought I was last getting out of the water. I was focused on swimming strong and was totally in my own head.

As we approached the last turn buoy back to the beach, I started to see more and more people swimming around me. I kicked it into gear and hurried quickly out of the water.

When the water became knee deep, I picked myself up and tried to run out of the water.

I ran on to the beach and into transition.

My biggest challenge—taking off my wetsuit!

But after I finally took it off and put on my sneakers, I ran out of transition and kept running until I was about a quarter-to-half mile into the run. I started at thirty–fifteen but I felt I could do more than that, so I ran a one minute fifteen seconds–fifteen seconds. I felt good.

Suddenly, I saw Monica. She was behind me. I thought she was out of the water and long past me by now. When she saw me, she kicked it into high gear and before long, she passed me.

We ran past the marina, then back to the parking lot, and to the nature preserve. I kept seeing Monica on the turn arounds.

On the way to the second preserve, I heard my name. Dawn and Danielle M. from my running team were screaming from a random car. It put a smile on my face. I wondered why they were in the car. Were they leaving? Coming? (I never did find out why they were in the car, but they stuck around until the end of the race.)

As I was heading toward the turnaround at the nature preserve, I took a fifteen-second walk break. "Yeah, catch your breath and walk around the turn," the volunteer said. I've gotten to the point where I'm used to these unnecessary comments. I gave him a thumbs up and started running after my fifteen-second break. He didn't say a word.

When I was close to the finish line, I could hear my teammates screaming my name. It was awesome to see them.

After seeing the results, I noticed I placed. I came in second. It was so exciting! And, in that moment, it reaffirmed my love for racing. Maybe I'm not as bad as I think I am? Maybe I'm okay at this? Maybe it doesn't matter, but when you place, it feels awesome!

I finished the 2019 season by racing with my running team at the Fall Foliage Race in upstate New York.

At every mile, I could see Joanne ahead of me. She was an amazing athlete and Ironman triathlete. I met her in Wildwood Warriors and just loved her. She was sweet, funny, and had a great smile.

Joanne was too far ahead to catch up, so I stayed back. At mile four, Joanne started to slow down, and I caught up to her. She wanted me to catch up so that we could take the rest of the half together. I was still in my "happy place."

At about mile six, the course started to change. There were lots of steep uphills and downhills. At around mile seven or eight, we started to see people coming back. "How far out are we?" I asked a couple running in the opposite direction.

"You're about a 1.5 to the turnaround," the woman shouted.

Joanne and I saw Bill, and we all ran together for about a half mile to a mile. Bill was taking it faster than I thought he would since the New York City Marathon, an event he'd been training for, at the time of the race, was just less than a month out. He passed us on the uphill and he was gone.

The course was tough. It was probably the toughest I had done. The hills were steep. But, as tough as it was, it was the most beautiful course I had ever done! They didn't call it Fall Foliage for nothing! The trees as well as the ground had gorgeous leaves on them—shades of green, yellow, orange, and red. The setting was breathtaking with the hills in the background and the colorful trees.

Although I lost my "happy place" on the uphills, I got it back on the downhills. Joanne and I just talked, laughed, and enjoyed the beauty of Rhinebeck!

After the race, we decompressed by going to a local diner to eat breakfast. I was starving! We talked about the course and laughed throughout breakfast. What an amazing course and a fun time! It was a great way to end the season.

The year ended with a great race, and my running group and I were already gearing up for 2020. We started to talk about next races and events. In December, I made a small holiday party at my home.

In addition to that, I went to a coaching camp in Clermont, Florida, to earn my coaching certification. It was an intense two full days, which consisted of everything swim, bike, and run. After the training, I read the manual and had to take a 100-question test. Thankfully, I passed with flying colors and became a certified USA Triathlon Coach!

Then, once I became certified, I had to continue my education by taking courses and earning credits to continue my certification. Everything was good. Things were looking bright, until we reached the new year.

Lesson Learned

Sometimes it's important to take a break from the mindset of triathlon races. Just enjoy the swim, bike, and run without the added pressure of competition. By doing that, you will either realize that you love this sport, or you don't. Whatever the case, taking a break can give you much needed perspective, and that's always a good thing.

2020

....

"I say two things to myself: Make it to the next aid station. Nothing beyond that matters. (Repeat.) and Stop running now, and the entire day/week/month is going to suck in your brain. You know it will. You'll be miserable. You'll pass people with medals, and you won't have one, because you stopped. Keep going until you get that f-ing medal."
–Peter Shankman, Ironman, New York

....

CHAPTER 32

COVID-19 Hits Us

JANUARY

Early in the year, my oldest friend, Philip, who I went to Camp Mikan/Recro with, committed suicide. That same day, I found out that another good friend, Stanley, had a massive stroke and was in a nursing home. It was horrible. I couldn't believe what was happening.

I had been with Philip a couple of months before. We had dinner together. He seemed in good spirits, and I loved spending time with him. He was like a brother to me. And, as for Stanley, he helped me so much when my kids were young. He would come over every weekend and bring them bagels, and we would laugh. He was a wonderful guy. Unfortunately, when I saw him, he didn't know what was going on. It made me so sad. I was distraught and depressed.

That's why I decided to run a half marathon every month in 2020. I couldn't let these negative experiences take over. I needed to focus on something positive.

I had six scheduled half marathons from January to June. I figured I would schedule the rest throughout the months that followed.

I also had a couple of smaller triathlons—Olympics and sprints lined up and was going to do a Half Ironman relay in Montauk in September.

I wanted to do the swim portion; Bill would bike, and Irem would run. I thought it would also be nice, since Ray was doing his first Half Ironman there, that we would all be there to support him. The relay and the half distance Ironman took place at the same time.

Also, during the month, my daughter's boyfriend, Dan, asked to meet with Brian and me for dinner. When we went out with him, he asked us for our daughter's hand in marriage. We were thrilled!

JANUARY AND THE DISNEY HALF MARATHON

I never ran a half marathon at Disney. In 2011, Becky and I were supposed to run the Disney Half Marathon, but when we got to Disney, we were both so sick. We forfeited the medal and went shopping instead of running. Then there was the Princess Half Marathon. I signed up for that with my two running partners, Didi and Colleen. It turned out I was unable to do that one also because I broke my toe.

I wanted to do the 2020 Walt Disney World Half Marathon, but it also gave me an excuse to see my son, who had recently relocated to Orlando.

I split a room with Didi, who was a big Disney fan. She was a slim, blonde-haired woman who looked amazing in anything she wore, including Mickey ears. I totally adored her. She was fun, smart, and knew her way around Disney, like the back of her hand.

Didi had done the 10K race that Friday. On Saturday, I needed to get up at 2:30 a.m. to catch the bus at 3 a.m.

Although the bus driver got lost at first, we got to the start line with plenty of time to spare. There was a significant walk from the drop-off site to the corral start lines. It was approximately a mile walk.

I got to the corral early and had about forty-five minutes before the race to try to get a spot close to the front. It was difficult, so I stood where I landed.

The runDisney races had a fantastic start. Donald Duck shouted, "five, four, three, two, one," and then fireworks went off. We ran through the gate. It was exciting. Everyone had a smile on their face.

Most of the race took place on the roadway and backlots of the Disney property. I went over and under bridges. Along the way, there were many characters. It seemed like almost every Disney character was on the road in various spots. You could stop and take a photo if you wanted to wait in line.

The other unique thing *run*Disney had was movies. They had a big screen set up in at least two spots along the route with Disney cartoons.

There were thousands of people running, and you felt it. It was hard to run at times because the roads were particularly narrow, and I felt like I was constantly getting bottlenecked. It was frustrating, and I wondered how the *run*Disney folks could have handled it differently, maybe accepting fewer people? Spreading people out more? I'm not sure, but it really needed a revamp.

At the end of the race, my son met me. I was so excited and thrilled to see him there. It had been a long while since I had seen him last and having him at the race made me so happy.

After the race, Didi and I drove down to Fort Lauderdale. Didi had a couple of days off before her half marathon in the Keys. I wanted to spend time with my dad.

When we got there, we found out dad's girlfriend had died. My dad's Alzheimer's was getting worse, and he barely remembered he had a girlfriend. Didi, my dad, and I spent a day at Butterfly World and then had a lovely dinner with Ed and Andrea.

FEBRUARY AND THE DONNA HALF MARATHON

There's something special about running a race through neighborhoods. I've done it a few times and each time was more special than the next. The 13th annual DONNA Half Marathon, in Jacksonville, Florida, was no different. This was a race that Dawn wanted desperately to run, and I wanted to support her. When I met Dawn in 2017, she was battling breast cancer. Thankfully, she was five years cancer-free at that point. The DONNA Half Marathon was to support those who had breast cancer and provide research for a cure.

The start was at the Beaches Town Center by AIA and 3rd Street. Dawn and I started together but within five minutes or so, we lost each other. I wasn't sure if she was ahead or behind me. I looked around and couldn't find her, so I plugged in my headphones and followed the crowd for 13.1 miles.

The race started at Neptune Beach. It went through various neighborhoods by the beach. Each neighborhood was so incredibly welcoming.

Talk about a block party! Atlantic Beach had chalk drawings that were motivational and uplifting. While Ocean Boulevard had palm trees made from green and pink balloons. It looked incredible. As I was going through the neighborhoods, a little girl with a "pussy cat" hat gave me a high five.

The neighbors were so warm and friendly. Many of them were giving out water, oranges, ice pops, and more. You could feel the love.

As I ran, I saw peeks of the ocean.

I kept noticing my time. My focus was on staying within a twelve-minute mile the entire way and, for most of it, I did. I kept thinking that I would see Dawn, but I never did.

As always, the last three miles were rough. I started to slip a little while trying to stick with the 2:40 group. My thirty–fifteen run–walk pace was held throughout. I felt good but I started to cramp up a little.

My son will be at the finish line, I kept thinking to myself. That motivated me to keep going. I knew I was almost there. I looked for him but didn't see him.

I turned the corner and saw the finish line. As I ran, I could feel it getting further and further away. "I got this," I said to myself. "I'm doing this for Dawn and the other survivors in my running group. If they could get through their cancer battle, the least I can do was finish this race in their honor."

After I crossed the finish line, I realized that I PR'd this half by four minutes. That was exciting. It was exciting to hear that Dawn also PR'd the race. A perfect end to a great race.

Total Time: 2:45:00

MARCH

I decided that it was time to hire coach, Danielle, back. We had a bit of a strange "break-up." I didn't know if I hurt her by leaving, but I was going through so much in my head. I still couldn't believe that my sister was not around. I felt such a loss.

I asked Danielle if she would take me back. I wasn't sure if she would. But she did, no questions asked, and we started training again. I still wasn't sure where I was going and what I was doing, but I knew I needed to have some structure and she was able to provide it for me.

COVID-19

Since February, we were hearing about a virus that came from China called the coronavirus. It was deadly, and people were dying in China. The White House administration told us that it wasn't coming here and not to worry. When I flew back from Jacksonville, I wiped down the airplane seats with disinfectant. I was worried.

By March, it was in New York full force. Our governor told us it came from Europe, but the president told us it came solely from China. There was so much misinformation in those early days and continued for years to follow. Our death rate in New York was growing rapidly, and the governor shut us down. We were on lockdown.

Sadly, I knew a lot of people who died, including an artist friend, an uncle, my girlfriend's parents. I also knew a lot of people who got it and are still suffering from long-term effects.

It was horrible and scary at the same time. No one wanted to leave the house, and if we did, all we could do was go to the supermarket or the drug store. Supplies were scarce. It was hard to get toilet paper, paper towels, hand sanitizer, and masks.

Everything else was shut down—restaurants, bars, theater, movies, concerts, and even races, both running and triathlon. So many people either lost their jobs and the economy was collapsing. No one knew what to do.

NYC HALF MARATHON CANCELLATION

A few days before the NYC Half Marathon, I got an email saying that they were canceling the race due to COVID-19.

Instead of being upset, I thought we could do it virtually and help everyone in the group look forward to something. I, for one, needed to do something for my mental health. I spoke with Ray, and at that point, I made him Assistant Coach of the team. We came up with a course starting at Cedar Creek, going to Jones Beach, up the boardwalk, until we reached 6.5 miles and then back. It was an out and back with a little extra in the park at the end.

I called New York Road Runners and asked if my group ran the NYC Half Marathon locally, would we still get the t-shirts and medals? They said, "Yes." Monica went into the city and picked up all the packages.

I thought this would be just perfect, especially since Danielle M. was running her first 13.1.

I sent out an email and about ten people showed up.

The part out to Jones Beach was fast and felt good.

As I got to Jones Beach, Ray stood and waited to direct the runners. He really is a special person! He shouted, "Make a right."

I started to see a couple of the members on the way back. I still felt great. I was in my happy place watching the beach with the waves breaking against the shore. It was spectacular.

Of course, I got a little lost and didn't make the turnaround. So, I had to double back. I passed the point, then the Jones Beach theater. I only had four miles to go.

Those were the hardest four miles. At that point, I dumped my sweatshirt. I tossed my pink long-sleeve shirt and was running in a short-sleeve tank with a jacket. I was absolutely freezing.

The wind was fierce as we came back in. All those negative thoughts that you try to push out of your mind came back to me. I was going at least a minute or more slower during those last few miles and was getting down on myself. I couldn't push through it. The wind was not my friend. But, seeing all my real friends on the course, pushed me to continue.

I needed to do this for everyone out there who struggled with finishing this race.

Unfortunately, those last four miles killed my PR. But that was okay. You can't predict conditions just like you can't predict what happens in your life. Nor could you predict that the New York Road Runners would cancel the event due to the influx of COVID-19. I was just happy to be outside running.

When I finished, I thought, "What an awesome way to run the NYC Virtual Half Marathon."

Lesson Learned

When things don't go the way you expect, be flexible, and reinvent the situation.

CHAPTER 33

Lockdown

After the virtual race, I tried to keep the team together. I had virtual meet ups every week just to see that everyone was still getting out of their homes to run, just a little bit. I tried to keep myself sane by cycling in the house, weight training, and running outside. Everyone was depressed, and I wanted to help.

The quarantine, which was supposed to last for only two weeks, lasted for months. Finally, I called Ray and said, "We need to get everyone together. I think we will all lose it if we don't run together." He was skeptical but participated, and I tried to get everyone to come together. Many of the folks didn't want to come out because they didn't want to wear masks. Others didn't want to show for fear of getting COVID-19.

Ray said, "There's nothing we can do so let's just move forward."

And that's what I did. I started the group back up in June and we continued to run together weekly. Those who joined us, great. Those who didn't want to, that was okay too; I tried not to take it personally but running certainly helped my sanity.

APRIL

I didn't expect to run in solitary on my birthday. I was anticipating going down once again to gorgeous Saint Petersburg and competing in the St. Anthony's Triathlon. Instead, with COVID-19 and the lockdown in New York, I stayed home. Depression set in, but I tried to brush it away. I tried to focus on what I had and not what I lost. I ran a birthday run around the neighborhood.

It was our scheduled run with my running group. I asked the group to run 5.8 miles in celebration of my fifty-eighth birthday. I was going to run in a park, but instead, I ran around the neighborhood. The miles went by quickly.

During the run, I noticed some interesting things. For starters, there were lots of drawings of rainbows on many of the homes. I figured that it may have been an assignment for school. But then, I realized yes, it could have been, but what made me go down this block to see them? My mother . . . When I see rainbows, I think of my mother. I smiled. She was wishing me a happy birthday.

As I was getting closer to my home, I saw a bunch of balloons outside someone's home. I smiled again. Balloons for Lori and me?

When I got into the house, I quickly showered and changed to get ready for my virtual running group call. We all talked about our runs, and it was just great seeing everyone. Of course, they all wished me a happy birthday and that made me smile.

After the Zoom call, I walked into the kitchen and lit a candle for my beautiful sister who shared a birthday with me. It was such a magnificent day, and I know she would have loved it.

My husband made the family pancakes, and we opened a bottle of champagne. We toasted to my sister and me.

After that, we sat on the couch and started to watch TV. Suddenly, a YouTube video came on and it just lit up my world. It was so special. My kids had recruited family, friends, and many of my runners to wish me beautiful birthday wishes, since I was unable to see anyone in person.

What a beautiful day. It may have been one of the best birthdays I had in years.

SWIMMING IN THE OPEN WATER AFTER ALL THE POOLS WERE CLOSED ...

Since all the pools closed with the lockdown, Ray and I decided to go to Tobay and attempt to swim.

When last year's season ended, I shampooed and stored my wetsuits, so they were nice and clean. When I took it out of the closet before getting into the car, the wetsuit smelled so fresh!

I packed my:
- Thermal wetsuit
- Swim cap and goggles
- Nose plugs and earplugs
- Towel
- Float buoy
- Water shoes.

I kept double-checking myself as if I were competing in a race. Do I have X? Do I have Y? Do I have Z?

Putting on the wetsuit was a trip! I forgot how hard it was to put it on. It was difficult with the few pounds I gained during the COVID-19 lockdown—those fifteen-plus pounds came right back on! But although I gained weight, I was excited to get back into some normalcy. I had the thermal wetsuit with me because I knew the water was in the low sixties.

I put on my booties and got all geared up and went in the water. It was freezing! "Hmm . . . I wonder if it will warm up?" I thought to myself. It didn't.

At first, I started to just float. Then, I took my first stroke. I hadn't swum since March 1st, three months ago! I took my arm out of the water and tried using my lats to take as big a stroke as possible. My hand entered the water, but the pull just wasn't right.

I took a few more strokes. My heart was beating out of my chest. My face was freezing, and I couldn't get myself to breathe the right way. I was holding my breath. "Relax," I thought.

As I tried to move forward, I kept feeling like I forgot how to swim. I could barely pull as my hand entered the water. How could I forget to swim? It's only been three months!

It seemed like Ray wasn't having as much trouble as I was. I felt like I was hyperventilating. Why didn't I take my inhaler before getting into the water?

We swam back and forth along the beach. We went about a half mile and then stopped.

I felt disappointed, but I knew it would get better from there. I started to think about every season that I've been in the open water, and it's always rough in the beginning. This was particularly rough because we hadn't taken a stroke in months. I knew before long I would get it back.

A few days later, we went out again. This time, the cold water on my face didn't feel as bad as it did on that first day back. We decided to swim back and forth along the beach again just to get back into it. I wore fins this time so that it wouldn't feel as hard, and I could practice on my stroke.

It went a little better than the first day, but still, I wasn't happy with my progress. I couldn't believe how hard it was and for me—swimming was my strongest part of the triathlon. After speaking to other triathletes including my coach, I tried not to be so hard on myself, which is always difficult since we are all our worst critics.

By the third time we went out, it felt better. The water was just as cold. Sometimes, there are so many mosquitoes there. On this swim, the bugs were eating us alive. But, I was swimming better. The current was little to none. The water was flat. Ray and I swam back and forth. My stroke was still a little off, and I realized I needed to focus on my breathing but, besides that, it was perfect!

****

Lesson Learned

Try to go with the flow. Life will hand you lemons and, when it does, try to make yourself some sweet lemonade!

CHAPTER 34

Training During COVID-19

Athletes have setbacks. There is nothing we can do about it. It's frustrating, and it happens when you least expect it to.

I was all set to do two major breakthroughs that year—a two-mile swim on Sunday and a forty-mile bike on Monday. Sunday came and I completed the swim with no issues. I felt like I could have gone longer!

The forty-mile bike ride scared the heck out of me.

But I kept thinking about a friend who I met through triathlon training. Her name was Staci. I saw Staci a week before riding Tobay. She had the biggest smile on her face. I noticed that many of the other riders were smiling too, and I wondered if they knew something I didn't know. Whatever the case, her smile stayed with me, and instead of being nervous, I enjoyed that ride.

Monday came, and after getting dressed, having my coffee, and my banana mash (a combination of mashed bananas and protein powder), I started to cough. My chest felt tight, and my throat felt as if it were closing. So, I decided not to do the ride and return to bed. It was a long weekend filled with my daughter's engagement party and the two-mile swim. It also included me driving my daughter and her fiancé back to New York City. Maybe I was just tired?

Monday night, I got myself ready. Two of my water bottles were filled. I had a couple of gels in my back pocket. I was set.

Tuesday morning came, I had my morning ritual, went out the door, and into the car. My bike had been in the car since the weekend. I was ready.

I drove over to Cedar Creek Park, unloaded the gear, and instead of standing over my bike overthinking the ride, I just went. I felt good. The wind was against me going out to Tobay. But it wasn't as bad as it could have been. I was happy and knew it would be okay. "You can do this," I said to myself. I smiled as I thought of Staci with her big smile. I love to ride; it's an awesome sense of freedom.

I got to the end of Cedar Creek and saw Jones Beach Theater. I always find riding around the bend toward the Tobay bike path tricky and go particularly slow there. As I went up a small incline to the Tobay path that led to the beach, I was feeling confident.

I rode four miles. I went through a barrier that blocked the opening to the beach with ease and circled the parking lot.

Just as I went up the gate to continue my ride, I caught on to something, and I banged into the rail. I'm not quite sure how it happened, but I felt myself go down, and my hip and my wrist took the brunt of my fall.

With no one around, I had to get back on my bike and ride back to Cedar Creek. It was painful. I had a hard time shifting and a hard time braking. I just wanted to get back to my car and go to urgent care. I had damaged my wrist three times in the last couple of years, I didn't want to take any chances.

After painfully loading my car back up, I drove myself to my local Urgent Care Center. I waited a few minutes, and the technician gave me an X-ray and found that I had sprained my wrist. I didn't even have anyone look at my hip. The COVID-19 weight gain padding helped with the impact!

Lesson Learned

If you fall, and you are down, get back on the saddle! Keep telling yourself you are stronger than a fall. Some days it works, and some days it doesn't, but keep on trying!

CHAPTER 35

Building Up Endurance

I was feeling optimistic, so I signed up for the Maggie Fischer Memorial Cross Bay 5.5-mile Swim from Fire Island to Bayshore across the Great South Bay. After not being able to swim in the pools for months and first getting into the open water in June, I realized pretty quickly that I was not ready for such a long swim. The event would end up being canceled because of the weather, but I knew I still wanted to try to become a marathon swimmer.

I WAS ON A MISSION TO BUILD MY SWIM ENDURANCE.

In mid-June when the weather started to warm up, Ray and I wore our wetsuits because the water was cold. I wore a long-sleeve wetsuit. When the water started getting warmer, I changed the long sleeve to the no sleeve. In July, after the second time wearing the no-sleeve wetsuit, I decided to not wear a wetsuit anymore. I felt like it was holding me back. So, for most of the summer, I just wore a bathing suit in the open water and loved it!

Each week, Ray, and I would build up our endurance. We started with 500, then 1,000, then slowly increasing to 1,500 yards, etc.

When we finally got to one mile, I smiled. I felt like I was back to where I was the year before. But on this day, we swam 3,650 yards. That was a little over two miles!

It's funny what kinds of things you think about when you're swimming in the open water. Crazy thoughts go through your mind like, "Do sharks come on the bay side?" or sometimes, you even hear noises like people talking when no one is around!

It's not just the meditative swinging your arms in the water, pulling the water, and breathing, it's also random thoughts. It's almost as if you are dreaming.

Then reality sets in and you think, "Where is that buoy?" or "How far to the next rest stop?"

I tried to refocus myself and count the strokes, one, two, three, four, five, six. I tried to get to ten, but I looked up after six, and that's a good thing. On this swim, I heard my training partner say, "Hilary, you're going in the wrong direction!" I was. I was swimming toward the opening of the inlet. I readjusted myself and swam forward.

During the two-mile swim, I couldn't tell how hard the current was, because it was always hard. I just did not think about it. I tried to get into a rhythmic motion and forget about life. That was the goal anyway!

Ray said, "That was my longest swim." I told him it was mine as well. Swimming made me feel alive. It gave me a sense of accomplishment. I felt as if I could have kept going. But it was enough.

I gave him an elbow bump to show him how proud I was of both of us for this accomplishment.

Lesson Learned

Don't ever forget to put Vaseline or Aquaphor on your body, especially under your arms and on areas where you will chafe. I forget every year, but starting today, I will put a sticky note on my closet, and so should you!

CHAPTER 36

Half-Distance Aqua Bike During the Pandemic

Since races had been canceled because of the pandemic, my running group and I decided to hold a "do it yourself" race. We called it the Festival of Things (FoT).

The FoT gave everyone the option to do something out of their wheelhouse. It was a time to celebrate life and to enjoy the beautiful outdoors before we got cooped up again.

THE PLAN

- Ray planned on doing a 70.3 half distance triathlon (1.2-mile swim, fifty-six–mile bike, and a 13.1-mile run = 70.3 miles)
- Irem, Jon, and Trish planned on a marathon. I believe it was Trish's first one
- Monica planned on an Olympic Triathlon. Her first one!
- The rest of the group did either a 10K or a seventeen-mile bike
- I decided to do a half distance Aqua-bike (1.2-mile swim and fifty-six–mile bike).

2020 HALF IRON AQUA BIKE

I didn't originally plan on doing a half distance Aqua Bike. I spoke with Danielle and asked her what she thought. She was excited. I wanted to step out of my comfort zone and get stronger on the bike.

Since I had been training with Ray for the 1.2-mile swim, I felt confident that I could do that. We swam more than two miles and it felt easy to me. I knew I was ready.

THE NIGHT BEFORE THE FoT

Ray organized the swim, bike, and run course. I sent around information to anyone on Long Island who was interested. I opened it up to other triathlon groups as well as the WeREndurance group.

That night I couldn't sleep at all. I kept thinking about the course. I was nervous, anxious, and excited all at the same time. If I could do this, I could compete in a Half Ironman event. I've been trying to do a Half Ironman event for the last five years and something always stopped me from doing it. I wanted to prove to myself I could get it done.

Ray and I arrived at Tobay Beach at 6 a.m. Thankfully, the bathrooms were open! As we got settled, I noticed another team there. The other team had music going and it seemed like a lot of people. Turned out, this other team had four people competing in a Half Ironman distance that same day.

"That is so funny," I said to the coach. "We are doing it, too!"

Ray and I got our swim stuff together and, before we knew it, we saw Dawn and Danielle M. It was incredible to see them there at the swim start. It made my day. Just as I was telling them how grateful I was that they were there, in walked Monica. I was shocked and excited at the same time. Monica was going to swim with us during her first leg of the Olympic Triathlon.

Following Monica was my coach, Danielle. I was so honored to have her there. It really meant so much to me!

Once we had our wetsuits on, I said to Monica and Ray, "Good luck to you . . ." and I started the swim. There were no guns, no swim start, just a "Do it yourself" event.

I always get out of the gate fast because I'm usually cold. Once I warm up, I get into a rhythm and feel very confident in the swim. I had so much energy and felt myself swooping the water with my arms and propelling my body forward.

I wore headphones and listened to the Silversun Pickups, a popular alternative music band.

On some days at Tobay, the water and the sky were the same color gray. It gave the illusion of a "white out." Sometimes, I felt that way when I skied and both the sky and the ground were white. You almost couldn't tell where anything started or stopped. Although on this swim, the sky and the water were the same, it made me smile. I think I smiled the entire swim.

"Why couldn't the swim go on forever?" I thought.

The buoys seemed to come up faster than I wanted. I felt like a kid on a roller coaster saying, "I want more!"

When I finished my 1.2-mile swim, Coach Danielle greeted me. "You did well," she said, "You did that 1.2 miles in fifty minutes. Great job."

She mentioned that Ray had finished nearly seven minutes earlier and was on his way to T1. Monica was still in the water, but I knew she would catch up on the bike and the run.

I got into my car, after being totally scraped up from the wetsuit, having forgotten to put Aquaphor all over my body. I followed Danielle to parking lot #6 at Jones Beach.

SWIM COURSE: 1.2 MILES, 50 MINUTES

T1—Jones Beach Parking Lot #6

I tried to get as organized as I could, but it was difficult having to transition out of my car. The bike came out first, and I started to get myself ready for the ride. I said to Danielle, "This is now the hard part." I gave her a smile.

I rode out onto the path. I was headed to Cedar Creek and made three loops and then added a couple of extra miles to make up the fifty-six miles.

I knew the bike course would be crowded but it wasn't terrible. There were plenty of people on the course, which slowed me down a bit. I didn't care. I just focused on getting it done. A few times during the first seventeen miles, Coach Danielle caught up with me. Her being there, just gave me the confidence that I could do it. She gave me pointers as I rode, and they were very helpful.

When I went out to Tobay, after my first lap, there was a headwind. She found me and told me to "keep aero." On the second loop, I tried staying aero the entire time in that section and in the third loop, I went even faster than the first and second loops.

As I was cycling, I saw Ray several times going in the opposite direction. He looked so happy. I was excited for him to do his first half distance. I knew he really wanted to do the cancelled Mighty Montauk half-distance race.

On the bike course, I saw my marathon group a couple of times as well. They looked strong. It was exciting to see everyone on the course.

When the computer got to fifty miles, I yelled out loud, "I just got to a half-century ride!" People around me looked at me as if I were crazy, but I was used to it because when I rode alone, I would also sing aloud.

At fifty-one miles, I was done. I had no nutrition or hydration left so I went back to the car. I saw Monica. She had just finished up and I congratulated her. I was so proud of her for doing the Olympic. That was a huge accomplishment.

I ate a bar and drank electrolytes with water. I was determined to finish the last five miles. I went out 2.5 miles and then on the way back in, I met a guy named Steve. He was a good rider. We were riding together, and I told him that I wanted to ride fifty-six. "Where are you at now," he asked. "55.5 miles," I said.

I was almost there. Just as I made it to fifty-six miles, I saw Ray. I yelled out, "Fifty-six miles baby! YAY!"

Steve turned to me and smiled. I told him that he now is part of my journey to fifty-six miles, and I thanked him.

BIKE COURSE: 56 MILES, 4 HOURS

When I finished, I saw Monica again. She told me she was leaving because she had a prior commitment. As soon as she left, I saw Danielle M. We set up some towels and a chair and hung out on "tar beach," a parking area where tar covers the ground. We could have gone to the real beach, but I think we both wanted to watch as our team members came in.

Irem and Jon came in soon after, and we just sat on towels in the Jones Beach parking lot. We talked and laughed. Ray came in, but he wasn't finished. "I have four miles to go," he said.

At that point, Irem and Jon left. Danielle and I stayed to see Ray come in. We sat for another hour, but we didn't see him so we both left. I was done. I needed a shower ASAP! Danielle M. continued to make me laugh since she's great at that. Before departing, we put a note on Ray's car to tell him we left.

As I sat and reflected on the day, I had a big smile on my face. Sometimes I forget that I really could do whatever it is I set my mind to do, thinking of my grandfather's mantra, "Shoot for the stars." It definitely resonated with me.

I never thought I would get to fifty miles that year, and I never thought I would do a half distance Aqua Bike. But I'm glad I did. It was an awesome experience, especially since it was a "do it yourself" race. It made me think that I could do a Half Ironman event. I had been so scared of that event for so many years, and yet, when there were no races on, I was able to complete it. I felt proud of myself for accomplishing this goal.

Lesson Learned

When you expect things to go one way, sometimes it doesn't. Things will always be out of your control. The COVID-19 pandemic threw everyone for a loop. We made the most of it. Adapt, adjust and just be patient. Things always turn around.

CHAPTER 37

Still Swimming in the Open Water

I've done some crazy things in my life, like crashing Woody Allen's New Year's Eve Party, skiing the Alps, wearing Google Glass in Costa Rica, and competing in dozens of triathlons. But on this day in mid-October, when the air temperature was fifty degrees Fahrenheit and the water temperature was 58 degrees Fahrenheit, swimming in the open water was one of the craziest things I had done.'

I didn't know if it was because of COVID-19 that I didn't want to stop swimming once the swim season ended, or if it was me going through a serious mid-life crisis, whatever the case, even when the water was freezing cold, it was truly glorious.

I wore so much clothing I could hardly move. My thermal wetsuit enabled my arms to move, but everything else felt heavy. I put in my earplugs and covered my head with the tightest hoodie. Once it was on, I could not hear anything. I saw people talking but I just saw their mouths moving. Nothing was heard.

I had my thermal socks on so when I got into the water, I didn't feel the cold. I felt as if I was in a big bowl of loose Jell-O. It felt thicker than the air and if, for example, I couldn't see, it would be hard to tell it was water.

My waterproof thermal gloves gave me a strange sensation. I felt the water around me, but it didn't seep in. It was a strange feeling.

I was totally bundled up, and the only thing exposed was my face. I jumped into the water and tried to keep my head out. When I took a stroke, it felt as if I was pulling an elephant through the water."

At the end of October 2020, I did it again. I swam with Ray and Nigel after work. They were so far ahead of me, but I stayed focused. I didn't care, I was in my happy place, focusing on the stroke. I tried to keep my arms at ten and two but that felt hard. It was amazing how easy it felt when I was in the pool! In addition to that, I tried to focus on my breath. My asthma kicked in and I could hear myself wheezing. It was just from the cold water.

When we all got to the first buoy, the guys waited for me. We snapped a photo. Then, we went to the marina. The current was with us going to the marina, which was nice.

From the marina to the middle buoy seemed harder than the first two legs. I could barely see the middle buoy. It was getting dark. I could see the lights at Tobay Beach, and they illuminated in the water, but we were too far from the lights to benefit. The moon was already out, and we could see the sun setting in the horizon. It looked gorgeous.

As we drifted around the middle buoy, I started to think about how swimming just melted away all the stress of the day. I never thought that I would like swimming and here I was absolutely loving it. It made me feel like a bird flying around, or better yet, a fish exploring the entire ocean.

I had been working on a huge project with a strict deadline. Between that and feeling stressed about all the craziness going on between the election and COVID-19, I felt I needed a break. When I swam in the open water, I felt like I got that break. It helped me escape and stay focused.

Lesson Learned

Just because it's cold outside, doesn't mean you can't swim outside, bike outside, or run outside. Try it one day. I have a feeling you will love it, too!

2021

....

"I had a tattoo of my wife drawn on my forearm. I look at the tattoo during races when things get tough. Then when I get to the finish line, there she is waiting for me ♡!"
–Andrew Cosgrove, triathlete, United Kingdom

....

CHAPTER 38

The Year of Hope

The year 2021 started with hope. Hope that COVID-19 would go away. Hope that the vaccines would come out quickly. Hope that everyone would get the vaccines and we could go back to our "normal lives."

I joined a gym with access to a pool because the local municipal pools kept shutting down. I needed a pool and wanted to make sure I could get access, and the only way to do so was to pay the membership fees.

FEBRUARY

Danielle had a maintenance plan that she incorporated during COVID-19. I decided not to take a break. I needed to train for my physical and mental health.

In the beginning of my journey, I felt that I had to prove to everyone else and to myself that I could compete in triathlons. Now, my motivation was to challenge myself. Funny, when I asked Richie, my first coach, for his blessing on this book, he even said to me, "I'm surprised you stayed with it this long."

I always loved a good challenge. When I started my business from nothing and grew it to a million-dollar business, it was thrilling for me. I wrote two business books and that was difficult, but I did it. I juggled a bunch of jobs including motherhood, my PR firm, blogging, podcasting, and teaching and yet, I met those challenges with ease.

I guess I was always looking for something that I felt was a challenge to prove to myself that I can do anything I set my mind to.

In a crazy way, I liked competing. No, I *loved* competing. There was nothing like the excitement and energy of a triathlon. The setting up, the nerves, the challenge, it's one of the most exciting things to watch. I watched a few of these races, and got a boost of energy each time.

The other thing I loved about triathlons is how they push me outside my comfort zone. I wanted to do things that I had never done before, and that excited me.

Thinking about all these things, I decided to sign up for the Maggie Fischer Memorial Cross Bay 5.5-mile swim from Fire Island to Bayshore in the Great South Bay. I also signed up for the Half Ironman in North Carolina.

Now mind you, I had signed up for three Half Ironman events in the past:

- Once in 2017, Ironman Atlantic City—but I didn't do it. I wasn't ready. And, although my friends, including Becky, did it, I just didn't feel good enough about myself to train and get it done.
- Second time in 2018, when I signed up for Ironman Augusta 70.3. But I didn't go because my sister passed away.
- Third time in 2019 at Ironman Maine. I thought it would be awesome to do. I knew a bunch of people doing it, but then, between the hills, the rough cold water, and the iffy temperatures in Maine, I decided not to do it.

I just wasn't mentally ready to do any of these. But, completing the half distance Aqua Bike over the summer made me feel like I could do it. Maybe I could finally cross the finish line?

Lesson Learned

Give yourself time to be ready for the challenge. Trust your gut. You will know when you are mentally and physically ready to race.

CHAPTER 39

Life Back to Normal?

MARCH

My family and I got our COVID-19 vaccinations and, after that, I decided to take a trip to Florida to see my dad. My timing was impeccable. Dad had gotten pneumonia the weekend my husband and I went to see him. He had just come home from the hospital. My brother told me he wasn't going to make it. When I saw him that Monday, I felt the same way. He was curled in a ball, shaking. But the next day, he seemed to make a miraculous recovery and was sitting up and alert.

He seemed to get better every day that followed while I was in that week; I was grateful.

The hospital didn't want to release him unless he was on hospice. They told me that he should never go back to the hospital. I agreed and signed the paperwork. I kept feeling conflicted. Did I do the right thing?

I ran two days when I was in South Florida. The first day, I was having a bit of a mental breakdown thinking about my dad. The run became a walk, and I spent a lot of time looking at the water. This was something I did when I was a kid growing up in Long Beach. When I was upset, I would go to the beach and just watch the waves break against the sand.

The next run was better. My head was in a better place. I was seeing some improvement. When I went to see my dad, he smiled when he saw me. His face lit up. That made me feel good. Although he doesn't know my name, he felt familiar with me.

I was grateful that I had the opportunity to see him again and see his smile. It just gets me upset that COVID-19 happened. It really affected our elderly. They were shut out and because of that, they went downhill. That hurt!

APRIL

I did my first Functional Threshold Power (FTP) test on the bike. (FTP takes the average number of watts that a rider can sustain in a set time and acts as a current measure of fitness.)

I did the test on my indoor CompuTrainer, which enables my bike to be in a stationary position, and I rode Zwift, which is a virtual ride where I rode with people around the world in real time. For twenty torturous minutes, I went all out. And, to my pleasant surprise, my FTP went up from last year! I felt good about that and followed up with a short run.

LIFE GETS IN THE WAY

My daughter got engaged in March of 2020, and her wedding was scheduled for the beginning of June. So much was going on for me personally. I was concerned about Mindy because her husband suddenly passed away. My father was getting worse. And I was feeling stressed about work; I felt like I kept pouring money into the business and not seeing much of a return.

My coach always told me, "Life gets in the way." It sure does.

"April is the cruelest month," wrote T. S. Elliot. April is a cruel month. It was my birthday month. I turned fifty-nine, the same age as my sister before her tragic death. Talk about stress!

MAY

I flew to Colorado to spend a weekend with Mindy. We had a really nice time, and I think for a moment, she felt a little better. However, once I got home from Colorado, the training was in full swing for the 5.5-mile swim.

The training became very intense. When I got back, I swam four days a week for a total of 17,000 yards a week. Then, it went to five days and more mileage.

Memorial Day weekend I spent at the gym and in bed. I swam 3.1 miles on Saturday in the pool. That was tough. I watched as people swam a little and left. No one was in as long as I was. I kept thinking that if I had a fast-action camera, it would look so interesting with people coming in and out of the water. I stayed focused. I had to swim twenty laps, then nineteen laps, then eighteen laps, etc., with a thirty-second break in between. I was in the zone. Suddenly, instead of seeing people come and go, I was alone in the pool struggling to count the laps.

Lesson Learned

Don't get mad at yourself for daydreaming or losing focus. Things happen and, sometimes, when you train hard, you get the opportunity to work things out mentally.

CHAPTER 40

Lots and Lots of Swimming

JUNE

The month started out cold in New York. Ray and I went in on June 2nd, and it was cold, very cold. The temperature read fifty-nine degrees. We started out doing a Tarzan and then slowly put our faces in the water. At first, it was brutal. But once we started to get used to it, it wasn't that bad.

We went out again two more times. On the third time, I had a long swim. Danielle called for 2.25 hours. "Listen Hilary," she wrote, "if it's too cold, don't do it."

I had seven weeks until the Maggie Swim and I started to get nervous. Could I do this? I asked Derek to kayak because at this long-distance swim, you needed a support team to kayak alongside and offer hydration and nutrition. Would Derek be able to handle the kayak?

I decided to swim a two-hour and twenty-five-minute swim. Ray went in, too. I felt I needed to get into the water as often as possible so that I could compete in this race. I only had four hours to get in 5.5 miles. I needed to swim at least 9,625 yards to accomplish this.

Ray and I got to Tobay at 5:15 a.m. No one else was there. We were surprised since there was so much action on the Tobay swimming page on Facebook. There were usually dozens of people in the water.

I struggled on what to wear. I put on my new thermal top and my long-sleeve wetsuit. However, it was very uncomfortable. I decided to do what Ray did—wear a thermal under a sleeveless wetsuit.

It felt more comfortable. But I was hesitant about how it would be in the open water with the temperatures so low. We both put on our booties and our gloves and set out to do a two-hour swim. Well, it was supposed to be two hours and twenty-five minutes, but I wasn't going to tell Ray that.

Once in the water, I could feel the coldness circle around my exposed skin on my calf. I tried not to think about it. But the real shocker was getting fully into the open water. I dunked myself in and started to scream. "Maybe we should leave," I said to Ray.

He calmly said, "Whatever you want to do."

We went out about ten strokes doing a Tarzan. When I was ready, I started to dip my face in the water. It was cold. I started to get a burning sensation on my face and around my body. "Can I do this? My coach did give me an out," I thought. But I shook it off.

We went out another ten strokes, this time with our faces in the water. "What do you want to do?" Ray asked me.

I told him, "Let's keep going."

We arrived at the Bonsai tree and took a break. "So, what do you think?" Ray asked.

I told him, "Let's get it done." He was just along for the ride. His big race was in October in Montauk, so he was just following my lead.

We swam back and forth and back and forth. He sped passed me like I was standing still.

I started to get nervous. Can I do this 5.5-mile swim within the allocated time? Will I get pulled from the water?

Soon, 1,000 yards, became 2,500 yards. And 2,500 yards became 4,000 yards.

When we got to the marina for the third time, Ray said, "Let's quit. I have to get to work."

I felt a little disappointed because we didn't finish the workout, but I knew I was all beat up from the water. My skin was chafed and felt like it was on fire.

We got to the beach and did a high five. Mentally, I felt good. I felt like I could keep going but when I stood up, I was very dizzy. My equilibrium was off.

I took a hot shower and pulled the wetsuit off me. This was followed by the booties, the gloves, the thermal shirt, and my tri kit. As the warm water hit my body, I was screaming in pain. My whole body was chafed! I forgot to put on anything to alleviate the chafing.

I put my towel around me, and two other swimmers/triathletes were with us. I had to take off my tri kit and my bra. I couldn't stand it any longer.

"Being a triathlete is like how a woman is after having a baby," I said to Ray. "You just don't care. You do what you need to do and that's that."

Ray chuckled. When I mentioned to the other two swimmers that I planned on driving home in a towel. The woman said to me, "Don't get pulled over." The thought of having a police officer pull me over when I was bare naked under a towel made me laugh.

As soon as I got home, I took a real shower. The water was burning me. I slathered my skin with Zealios chamois cream, and the burns started to feel better. I was chafed all over my neck, my arms, under my arms, my belly. You name it, I was chafed there!

My husband said, "I just don't understand why you do this." And all I kept thinking was, "When is the next time I can swim in the open water again?"

FEELING NERVOUS

My daughter's wedding was the following weekend and my neck, back, and under arms were still all chafed and swollen. I spoke with Danielle, and she agreed that frequent short open waters and pool swims would be sufficient this week. "Don't worry," she said to me, "You're doing great."

But I still wondered if I would be able to make the cutoff. I was swimming around a forty-five-minute mile then, and the cutoff was four hours. Depending on the current, it could have taken me longer. I didn't know if it was going to be possible. I hoped so. I wanted to conquer this and, if not, at least I tried!

I was nervous about this event. Nervous about my daughter's wedding. And I was nervous about my body. As I mentioned earlier, I gained all the weight back and then some during COVID-19. Now, I was the biggest I ever was in my entire life, having gained twenty pounds.

I really didn't understand what was going on. I was working out, preparing for the swim almost two sometimes three hours a day. I was eating healthy, staying within my 1,600-calorie diet, and yet, I was gaining weight. It didn't make much sense, and it was frustrating me to no end!

I tried to brush away the thought of feeling so overweight. I could hear my mother saying to me, "Look at you. You look terrible!"

I wanted to focus on these events coming up. I needed to stay focused and visualize the finish line.

Lesson Learned

Don't go for a long swim, a week before your daughter's wedding!

CHAPTER 41

And More Swimming at Tobay

Zoey's wedding was wonderful. We had an amazing wedding weekend and sent the newlyweds off to Mexico for their honeymoon.

The Monday after the wedding, training was back in motion. At that point, I was swimming five days a week instead of four. I needed to train on the bike and the run. In addition to that, I needed to continue to strength train, all in preparation for the upcoming Half Ironman. There were a few days where I just swam and couldn't do anything else.

SWIMMING AROUND THE ISLAND

Every year, there were lots of groups who swam around the island at Tobay Beach. I did it once with Total Masters Swimming but hadn't done it again in years.

"Which direction do you want to swim in today?" Ray said to me as we got into the water. I pointed to the marina. I loved starting that way first because it's a longer, harder swim than going to the Bonsai tree.

"Why don't we go around the island to check it out?" I asked. He gave me a smile and we swam toward the island.

"Just don't swim too far away," I screamed after him. I didn't want to feel alone on the "other side."

We got to the other side of the island. I could no longer see the beach. I felt like I was now in the open water. I felt like Nemo, exploring new territory.

I noticed that Ray started to drift farther and farther out. I screamed his name. At first, he didn't hear me. But then he finally lifted his head and I waved to come closer to the shore.

We continued. I started to think about Krabby Patties, Patrick Star, and Squidward from *SpongeBob SquarePants*. I needed to think of myself as a crab as I pulled the water.

Between Nemo and Squidward, I visualized cartoons in my head.

Suddenly, a boat passed us. The captain stopped and said, "I saw buoys but didn't know what it was." I usually wear a pink or orange buoy so that I can be seen. He laughed. We laughed. Before we knew it, we were at the end and headed back toward the Bonsai tree.

When I got back from my swim, I saw a comment on Facebook, "Was that Hilary Topper going around the island?" Then someone else sent me a DM, "Was that you who went around the island?"

****

Danielle had another client that she was coaching for the long-distance swim, and she suggested that Katie and I swim together.

The first time Katie and I swam together was at the pool. We noticed that we were similar in speed. Then when we went to the open water, we noticed that we were the exact same speed. We swam side by side and it was incredible. It felt good swimming with her.

Katie and I went on all our long swims together, including a three-hour swim where we swam four miles! I was so impressed that we did it. But, during that last mile, my shoulder was starting to hurt badly.

SWIMMING AGAINST THE CURRENT

My son and I decided to go for a practice swim. He would kayak and I would swim.

I usually went to Tobay in the morning, but since he likes to sleep in, I went at 5:15 p.m. after work. By the time we got into the water, it was 5:30 p.m. I left my buoy off.

We blew up his inflatable kayak which took about fifteen minutes. Then, I helped him into the water. He wanted me to drag the kayak myself while he stayed in the boat so that he didn't have to get wet. But there was no way I could do it. My biceps were aching. So, he jumped out and helped me get the boat in the water.

Once he was in the water and floating, I slowly made my way in. The water was cold but not as bad as usual. When I was up to my chest, I went for it. I screamed for a moment, and then once I got moving, I got used to it.

We set out to the left of the beach toward the Bonsai tree. It took a while, but it didn't feel bad. The current felt about as normal as usual.

Derek stayed on the left of me, and it went smoothly. I took a sip of water from my water bottle on his boat, and I told him that we were going to go to the middle buoy.

Suddenly, a swarm of people jumped in the water and were heading our way toward the middle buoy.

Once we got there, I felt like I was being tackled by a lot of people. They were swimming back and forth from the middle buoy to the beach and back.

I could see that Derek was getting caught up with the people too. I motioned to him to go to the marina.

We flew to the marina. I don't think I have ever gotten there so fast. But I didn't think anything of it. We met up at the buoy closest to the marina.

As I stood there, I could feel the current push me toward the boats. It was strong.

"Wow, this is going to be tough getting back," I said to Derek. "I would suggest going as close to the shore as possible because there should be less current there."

He tried. He then yelled to me, "Don't worry about me, I'll get back. Just worry about yourself."

That wasn't happening. You know how mothers are, they worry about their children!

I headed back. I felt like I was in an infinity pool. The stronger I was going the more I was being pushed toward the marina. I couldn't believe it. This was the first time that I felt such a strong current there.

Getting an alert on my phone earlier in the day that there were rip currents didn't scare me. I figured they were only in the ocean. I never thought that it would impact the bay side in an inlet.

I struggled. I wasn't going anywhere, and my goggles were all fogged up. I couldn't see anything. I looked around and couldn't see Derek. I hoped he hadn't crash into one of the boats.

Finally, I saw him. He was on the beach by the marina. He motioned for me to keep going, but my arms were throbbing. I had enough and wasn't getting anywhere. I swam toward him.

We both looked at each other and decided to take the kayak back to the car. "We're not that far," I said.

He told me he had called his dad, and he was on his way to pick us up. When Brian got there, we threw the deflated kayak on top of his car, and he drove to the lot. I decided to walk on the beach path back to where the restaurants were located.

We had dinner at one of the Tobay Beach restaurants. They had two restaurants there. As we sat outside, I saw a woman I knew and said hi. "Did you go out there?" she asked me.

"Yeah, I got caught up at the marina," I said.

"We just stayed around the buoy because of the current. It was wicked," she said.

When I went on Instagram, I also saw other people who were also out. They were saying the same thing, "The current was no joke."

It was scary, and I just prayed that we would have a nice day at the July race.

JULY

Derek and I sat in on a mandatory meeting for the Maggie Fischer Memorial Cross Bay Swim. This was getting real. We were told that the weather would be on our side and that there would be a nice current behind us.

Derek and I put together a list of everything we needed. I went out and bought a dry bag and told him to set his watch for every 30 minutes so that I could get nutrition and hydration. We were set.

The Wednesday night before the race, we got word that a tropical storm was going to hit us on Friday morning and that the race organizers postponed the race until August 12th. This was the first year it was postponed.

After that, I reached out to Cathy and Katie, "Do you guys want to swim Tobay on Saturday morning at 5 a.m.?" I asked. They both responded that they were unable to join me. In the meantime, my friend, Thomas, reached out and said he wanted to swim five or six miles on Saturday morning. He told me he was going to reach out to his swimming friends and see if they wanted to join us.

When I arrived at 5 a.m. at Tobay Beach, I was thinking that if Thomas backed out, I would swim a few miles on my own. But, when I got to the lot, I saw Thomas waiting for me.

"Everyone else backed out," he said. "It's just you and me."

Knowing that he was a much faster swimmer than me, I told him I would wear my fins. (There's a push anyway at the Cross Bay, and Tobay had a lot of current.)

We went out at a relaxed pace and stayed there for 5.25 miles for me and six miles for him. Thomas zigzagged around me so that I always had him close by. That made me feel safe and comfortable.

When we finished, I felt so proud of myself. For someone who used to have major panic attacks in the water and couldn't swim twenty-five yards, I did great!

After the swim, I got a text message from Coach Danielle congratulating me. She got a notification that I finished.

I was a little nervous that I wouldn't be able to keep up with the swimming because Ironman training was starting. I had a conversation with Danielle. "Don't worry," she said. "You will be fine."

She explained that the long swims would only be once a week and that everything else would need to be worked in.

Lesson Learned

Races get cancelled. Sometimes portions of the race get cancelled, like the swim. Go with the flow, and if you can do it on your own, more power to you!

CHAPTER 42

Maggie Fischer Memorial Cross Bay Swim

Toeing the start line at the Maggie Fischer Memorial Cross Bay Swim was just the finale of a long five-month training period. It's funny looking back to the year before when Ray and I swam two miles at Tobay Beach. I was thrilled then! Now, I was extremely excited and ready to cross that bay.

ON THE DAY OF THE EVENT

Derek committed to kayaking for me during this race. He wasn't an experienced kayaker, and I knew that there may be some issues going into this event. We went out once or twice on his inflatable kayak, but he never kayaked in the open water. The inflatable kayak was only appropriate for lakes and ponds, not the open water. I frantically started looking to buy a kayak.

An Iron Fit Endurance team member graciously loaned Derek and me a kayak to use during the race. He dropped off the kayak at Bayshore and it was loaded on the ferry.

The race organizers arranged for the Fire Island Ferry to pick the swimmers and kayakers up in Bayshore and bring us to Fire Island.

Once there, we unloaded, registered, and waited for the boats to unload so that we could bring them down to the shore.

We all had about an hour to get ready and get into the water. Before the race started, Katie and I hugged and wished each other luck.

As the gun went off, so did the swimmers. I'm not sure what happened after that. I swam, looked around, and saw no one in the distance, just Derek on the kayak.

"Do you see where to go?" I asked Derek. He said he was following the people in front. But I still didn't see anyone.

Although we may have gone off course, the first two miles were uneventful. The water seemed mellow, and I was in my happy place. I wanted it to go on forever!

Then the water started to change and became very choppy and, with the chop, I couldn't see in front of me. The swells were incredibly high. I didn't know if we were going in the right direction. I couldn't see the buoys or the boats.

Suddenly, Dave, one of the volunteer kayakers came over to us, and he told me to follow him in. I told Derek to stay with us. He said that we were way off course and he would take us to where we should be. I started to follow him, and, with his bright colors, it was easy to spot him. Derek stayed by my side. He kept getting pulled out but then circled around and made it back.

When the race started, I turned on my Garmin to track the race. I never shut it off, even when I stopped to take in some gel. For some reason unbeknownst to me, the Garmin shut off for almost an hour, giving me this false sense of where I was at with the swim. I thought I had plenty of time. When I looked at my watch it said I was at two hours and forty minutes. But when I spoke with Dave, he said I only had an hour left, then twenty minutes left. I didn't know who to believe. It was very disorienting.

Between looking at my watch trying to find my distance, the chop being so rough, and my left shoulder in horrible pain, I was no longer in my happy place. There was supposed to be a current taking us to the beach. I felt nothing.

Derek was very helpful and kept offering me gels and hydration. But Dave was saying we didn't have long before the course closed and told me to keep swimming. I was worried we wouldn't make the cutoff. And yet, if we didn't, it would be okay because I already swam more than five miles with Thomas.

I kept trying to channel Maggie Fischer, the young woman in which the swim was named. Maggie was a high school swimmer who was going to swim this race, but a few weeks before it took place, she had a tragic car accident.

I knew she was there; I could feel her in the water. She had to be helping everyone get through this.

Throughout the swim, I kept feeling fish. I would feel fish nibbling on my fingers as I came in for the catch, gliding myself through the water. One time, when I was taking a good pull, I found myself hitting a big fish. It startled me. I looked around and saw Derek and continued swimming.

The other strange thing that happened was when I was between miles four and five, I entered a very salty patch. It was as if someone dumped salt right there in the water. I could barely breathe it was so salty.

I thought about quitting but that wasn't an option because I trained so hard. I wanted it.

The water was intense and choppy. I had been swimming for so long, and my shoulder stopped working. I had to start breathing out of my right side to alleviate the pain. It would have been easy to DNF.

"Where is the push?" I asked Dave, the kayaker. "Don't you feel it?" I didn't feel anything. I felt like everything was fighting me.

I looked over at Derek. He smiled at me. I was going to finish this! That smile was infectious. I focused on it and his smile helped get me through the race.

I was about a half mile from the beach and could barely see where I was going. Seeing two small beaches, I wasn't sure where to aim. Then I saw a finish line. I kept stopping and asking, "Where am I going?" That seemed to be the theme of this race . . . where am I going?

At that point, I had a parade of boats and kayakers surround me. Dave pointed in the direction of the finish line. I swam as hard as I could, and it was pathetic because at that point I couldn't move my body. The more I pushed the further I felt from shore. Derek offered me a gel and I shook my head. I had to finish. I had to do this . . . I only had a little bit more to go.

Finally, I got to the beach and was greeted by Shawn and Coach Danielle. Katie was also there, she finished about a half hour earlier.

All I could say as I got to the beach was, "That was the hardest swim I ever did."

Although my arms were barely working, I ran through the chute, struggled to lift my arms but managed to give a signature pose.

As I walked past Danielle, she said, "Don't leave, you're getting an award." I was so exhausted and collected my swag bag and my purchased t-shirts.

I grabbed half a bagel and some water and tried to organize my stuff. I felt disheveled, and I couldn't get focused.

Finally, I heard my name called and I went up for what Thomas called, "The Goober Award," but the Maggie Fischer folks called it the Endurance Award. I came in last place, but I didn't care. I finished the race and that's what I set out to do. Hey, every race should have a last-place award!

This one I had to dig real deep to finish, and I'm proud of myself for getting it done! It really was a huge accomplishment, especially from someone who only learned to swim six years ago!

One of the committee members reached out to me on Instagram and said, "The Endurance Award is the highest honor at the Maggie Fischer Swim. It goes to the most tenacious swimmer that sticks it out and achieves their goal."

Lesson Learned

Don't stop. You will cross that finish line, and you will be a winner!

CHAPTER 43

Half Ironman Triathlon Training

As soon as the Maggie Fischer Memorial Cross Bay Swim was behind me, I immediately started training for Ironman North Carolina 70.3. It was unfortunate because I didn't have a moment to think about the accomplishment I made. I had to get right into Half Ironman training, and it was intense!

My first week after the swim, I did the following:

- Saturday—Five-mile run
- Sunday—Two-and-a-half-hour bike
- Monday—One-mile swim
- Tuesday—Intervals on bike then thirty-minute run off bike
- Wednesday—Thirty-minute swim then thirty minutes of strength
- Thursday—Track workout
- Friday—One-and-a-half-mile swim and one-hour bike, followed by strength
- Saturday—Eight-mile run
- Sunday—Ninety minutes on the bike trainer of intervals in Zone two and three
- Monday—Finally rest!

The following week consisted of some very hard and long workouts, including a three-and-a-half-hour bike ride followed by a run. I knew I had to get these in, thinking that it would take me very close to the time limit to finish. I had eight hours and thirty minutes to finish a Half Ironman. I wanted to finish in eight hours and fifteen minutes!

THREE-AND-A-HALF-HOUR RIDE AND RUN OTB

Nine weeks before the event, I had a three-and-a-half-hour bike ride followed by a run off the bike. The run was short, only two miles, so I felt confident I could get it done.

Ray told me he would join me. We started out at 4:45 a.m. It was pitch black. Since the gates were closed, we went through the back entrance of the parking lot and parked the car close to the bike path. We both needed a restroom and, luckily, the family room was open, so we made a pit stop before heading out.

I was nervous. I had never ridden in the dark before, except for a couple of times when I had to ride to a triathlon transition area. But I never rode a trail before in the dark. A few days before the ride, I purchased a light for my helmet and a light for my bike.

I turned them on and started to head out. The heat wasn't bad at that point. It was still dark, and the air was slightly breezy. We had been experiencing a heat wave, and this was the last day of it.

At first, we went out slow. I think we were both afraid that we may ride over a bunny or a duck. Then, as the sun rose, we picked it up. My coach wanted me to ride in zone two and three the entire way. Everyone's zones are different, and they are based on the FTP test that I did during the winter. Zones can be done with heart rate, Rate of Perceived Effort (RPE), or they can be based on your watts. But it was breezier than anticipated, and the wind was either behind us or head on in spots.

The ride was uneventful. Ray left after one loop, which was thirty-seven miles. I still had another ten miles to go. As I was riding on the path, I noticed a young woman in a bra and tight shorts. "Dee?" I yelled. My coach calls herself "Dee."

"Oh, hi Hilary," she screamed, and with a blink, I had gone way past her on the bike.

I finished up the ride and rode back to my car, which was still parked at Jones Beach. I was stiff. My back was hurting. My butt was hurting. I stretched out a little, got my fluids for the run and started out onto the Jones Beach boardwalk.

I set my watch for fifteen-second run/thirty-second walk. I figured I would start there. I found it so difficult to run off the bike. My legs were wobbly from riding hard.

As I was running, I passed a woman I knew through triathlon training. She was running strong. She yelled out, "Looking good." But I wasn't feeling good. I was so hot and as I was running, I could feel my knee buckle up. Uh oh. That wasn't good. I only ran about a half mile and that was it. I went back to the car.

I couldn't run. How am I going to do this?

When I got home, I iced, compressed, and did everything in between for my knee. Talk about nursing an injury! I even used a TENS machine, a device that stimulates the muscles. I was so depressed. I wrote to my coach, who said, "Everyone gets injured. It's a fact of being an athlete. Don't worry, you have eight weeks."

She suggested that I get a refit on my bike. That's where the bike mechanic looks at you on the bike and sees if there are any issues. If there are, he adjusts. She also suggested that I go to a chiropractor for ART—Active Release Technique—where the doctor uses soft tissue mobilization to work out the pain in a particular area.

I did both. I went to the bike shop, and the owner spent a long time with me looking at my pedals and the way my foot was positioned. He also watched as I rode on the bike situated on a trainer so it wouldn't go anywhere.

He told me that I was favoring the right side of my body and that's where the problem was. So, he raised the seat, stretched out the aero bars, and leveled out the seat. "Okay, let me know what you think after you ride it," he said.

I went to see a chiropractor for the knee, and it started to feel a little better.

A couple of days later, I took the bike out for a spin. I didn't feel pain in my knee. I just rode easy. The fit felt good.

A few days after that, I had a track run. Since there was a tropical storm, I decided not to do it and ran around the neighborhood instead. I went out easy five-second run–twenty-second walk. As soon as I started, I felt the pain and pressure on my knee again. After about a half mile, I stopped. I felt like I could walk so I walked the 2.5 miles. I needed to build up the endurance for the 13.1 section of the triathlon. (If I can walk 13.1 miles, I can run it. Once this knee heals, I will be okay.)

I called another "back of the packer" who just finished Musselman 70.3. "Tell me what you did right and how long it took you to finish," I asked her.

"I raced through transitions, didn't talk with anyone on the run, and made it in at 8:20!" she told me. I was impressed.

"You need to practice transitions," she said. "And leave yourself enough time on the run so that you can make it in."

I took her advice to heart. I planned on doing more transition work and working on the other disciplines so that I could make it in.

After talking with my friend, I texted Coach Danielle and asked her what to do about peeing. "Just pee on the bike," she said.

What? Peeing on the bike? I couldn't even pee in the water. I needed to push to get it started. What if I pushed too hard on the bike, and I accidentally pooped?

I started asking everyone I knew if they peed on the bike. Most told me they did. Some looked at me as if I were crazy and said they stop.

After the peeing discussion, I ordered two sets of two-piece tri kits. If I'm going to stop in North Carolina, I need to pull down my pants quick and not struggle with the one-piece tri kit.

I thought I'm just going to have to go out as fast as I can to make up time for the run and make pit stops along the way!

Lesson Learned

Triathlon is not a glamour sport. Athlete's pee, poop, and puke on the swim, bike, and run. It's just part of the excitement.

CHAPTER 44

Training Continues

I went out with my running group since my knee was feeling a little better. We planned a nice long run at Heckscher Park,

There was a threat of rain that day. On my way out to Heckscher, there was a downpour. It was so bad at one point, I considered turning around, but I ran the group, so I felt obligated to attend.

During this run, Marc, Jodi, Jon, Ray, and I were there. Everyone else backed out because of the rain. When I got to the park, it was drizzling. Perfect weather for a long run!

We started out at ten-second run–twenty-five-second walk. Within a half mile, I was hurting bad. "Hilary, why don't you just walk. You're going to hurt yourself worse if you continue running," Jon said to me. He was right. I needed to stop.

As the group continued to go, I felt depressed. What's going on with my knee? How could I run the 13.1 miles of the Half Ironman if I couldn't even run a half mile?

Members of the group were wonderful. They waited for me at the parking lot. I finally got there, and Ray initiated a clap. They all started to clap for me. "Are you okay?" he asked me. I shook my head. I knew there was a problem, but I didn't want to admit it. My knee was burning with pain, and I had sciatica running down my leg.

They headed back out, and I sat in my car and started to cry.

GOING TO THE ORTHOPEDIC DOCTOR

There's a doctor in Manhattan at Hospital for Special Surgery that I went to about twelve years ago. At that time, I had recovered from meniscus surgery but still had pain. She focused on women's knees, and I felt confident that she would be able to fix me up.

This time when I got there, she looked at my X-rays and said, "I don't think you should run again."

"But I have a Half Ironman in October," I said whining a little.

"Can't you walk?"

"No, I wouldn't make the time cutoff."

She recommended an MRI, but because of insurance I had to wait a week for approval.

MY DAD

Meanwhile, my dad took a turn for the worse. The woman who owned the group home called me. She said my dad wanted to FaceTime me. I turned it on and told him I loved him, but he just looked at the phone as if it were a foreign object. She urgently told me to call hospice. "If you don't get them here, I'm calling the ambulance to take him to the hospital," she said.

The hospice staff evaluated him on Monday, September 6th. They called me and told me he was fine. "He's eating beef," the nurse said.

The next day, the woman who owned the home called me again. Again, she was in a panic. I called hospice, and they sent someone right away. This time, they told me he needed twenty-four-hour care in the palliative unit of hospice. I gave my consent, and he was taken to the facility.

My brother had just come back from Disney with his wife, and they both went to see him. He called me from the unit. "Hil, it's really beautiful here. It's a big room and a beautiful garden outside his window. They are piping in relaxing music," he said. "Dad's been sleeping since he got here. He hasn't opened his eyes, not once."

He started to tell me this was it and talked about the funeral arrangements in the room while my dad lay there, struggling to survive. "Ed, stop talking about this in front of dad. Put your phone in his ear," I commanded.

He did. "Dad, I love you so much. I just want you to know, everything will be okay. Daddy, I love you," I said.

At that moment, he opened his eyes and mouthed, "I love you too." Andrea told me she saw the whole thing.

"That was so special," she said.

My dad died the next day. He was eighty-eight years old and finally at peace.

I took a few days off from training while attending his funeral. I loved my dad so much, but the last few years had been difficult. It was hard not being able to see him during COVID-19, and by the time I did see him in Florida, he had no idea who I was. His disease put a lot of stress on me. There was one time when I was swimming in the open water and just started to cry in the middle of the water. I couldn't stop. But after his death, I felt somewhat relieved. I knew he was in a better place.

THREE DAYS LATER . . .

Still feeling emotionally drained from the funeral, I had to go back to the orthopedic doctor and get that MRI.

I drove into the city and met my daughter, who wasn't feeling well, for lunch, and, then went to the doctor. I had my MRI, and while I was in the machine, I thought, "My knee really hurts but I think it's just a sprain. I'll be okay. I know the doctor will tell me I'll be good to go for the Half Ironman."

After the MRI, I walked across a series of bridges that connected three buildings at the Hospital for Special Surgery. I went to her office. They called me in the back within minutes of my arrival.

The doctor walked in, "Wow, you must have a high tolerance of pain," she said. "You have a torn meniscus and a tab sticking out. You need surgery. We will take bone marrow from your hip and rejuvenate your knee."

She drew a diagram, but it all seemed way too overwhelming. My dad died earlier in the week and now this? Is this really happening?

"So, I'm going to have to cancel Ironman North Carolina?" I asked her.

She nodded her head, yes. My brain started to work in fast motion, and I have no idea what she said after that, something about using crutches and being in a brace for six to eight weeks. Within minutes, I was ushered to a scheduler who told me I could get the surgery that Monday or wait until mid-October. I opted to wait.

Lesson Learned

If this had happened to me five years earlier, I would have been traumatized. Although these last ten years have been brutal at times, I learned, developed, and grew. I now know what I am capable of, and this is just another bump in that road. I can walk away from this experience proud of myself and confident that I can and will accomplish what I want in the coming years.

I AM A TRIATHLETE AND ENDURANCE ATHLETE.

CHAPTER 45

Conclusion...

We all wish the road would be easy and everything in our lives go smoothly. However, this is not always the case.

The road will be bumpy. It's how we handle it and the attitude we have that will either make it worse or make it bearable.

I don't know if there is a perfect triathlon or endurance event. Every time I read other people's posts on Facebook with their race recap, it always sounds horrible. Yet, people endure.

Think about what you accomplished. Although you may not be able to accomplish everything, or maybe you did, be proud of yourself for taking that step in the right direction. As Coach Richie had told me, "Don't stress over the small stuff" and look at the big picture.

You are doing this for you and no one else. If you want to run a 5K and that's your big goal for the year, go for it. It's an awesome goal!

If you want to race in an Ironman triathlon and complete it, good for you! If you compete and don't finish, it's okay. You got to the starting line healthy. That's a huge accomplishment. And remember, there's always next year.

Look back and be proud of yourself. When I look back, I started as a non-athlete and now look at me. I'm a true endurance athlete, and you know what, I'm proud of myself.

If you don't have support in your life, use that lack of support and lack of belief in yourself as a motivator to push forward.

I am proud of you for reading this book and planning out your goals. You can do it!

Thanks again for reading about my journey . . . I'll be back after this knee surgery, and I plan on doing great things in my sixties and beyond. Hopefully, I'll even do that Half Ironman!

Looking back on my year in 2021, it wasn't a bad one. Yes, bad things happened. Bad things will happen. But as for training, I swam nearly two hundred miles, I biked nearly fifteen hundred miles, and I ran nearly three hundred miles. I am happy, and I am content.

When you look back, what did you do? If you got out there and ran a block, good for you! That's awesome, keep it up. If you ran a half marathon or competed in a triathlon of any kind, that's amazing. You are incredible. Continue to do great things.

Have a great day! But before you do so, stand up and give me that signature pose!

EPILOGUE

Now it's been almost three months since my meniscus surgery, and I'm feeling much better. I've continued to swim, bike, and strength train throughout the rehab process. I even went skiing in Colorado with my husband in early January. I was so excited that I was able to do that, even if it was only on the small-town hill.

Throughout the last ten years, I have battled my mental health demons, accepted and embraced the fact that I am a back-of-the-packer, and have used my love of endurance sports for the things that have been hard in life. I'm so happy that I found a good balance.

I am amazed at what I've accomplished even dealing with all the unexpected tragedies. I know the minute I jump in the ocean, lace up my sneakers, put on my helmet, the sport of triathlon will be there for me to help me process it all. I am strong and mentally ready to take on my next challenges.

This year, I have big plans. I plan on racing at St. Anthony's Triathlon again, swimming a two-mile ocean swim in Boca Raton, Florida, competing in a marathon swim in Ann Arbor, Michigan, racing the Mighty Hamptons again, and riding my first century ride. Let's see if I can make it all happen. And, if I can't, at least I tried.

I decided that the Half Ironman isn't in the books this year. I plan on building up my run, and one day I will get there. I just started to run a little bit. I'm taking baby steps to get back, but I will get back. For anyone who has been injured or who is currently injured, you will be back, too!

Remember, the road will be bumpy, but it will always be waiting for you.

Credits
Cover and interior design: Anja Elsen
Layout: DiTech Publishing Services, www.ditechpubs.com
Cover photo: Ed Grenzig of LIRP Long Island Running Photos
Managing editor: Elizabeth Evans
Copy editor: Sarah Tomblin, www.sarahtomblinediting.com